MY FOWL LIFE

*Misadventures with Chickens
and Guinea Fowl*

LAURA LEE CORNWELL

authorHOUSE®

AuthorHouse™ LLC
1663 Liberty Drive
Bloomington, IN 47403
www.authorhouse.com
Phone: 1-800-839-8640

Published by AuthorHouse 11/14/2013

ISBN: 978-1-4918-3615-6 (sc)
ISBN: 978-1-4918-3614-9 (e)

Library of Congress Control Number: 2013920595

Dedicated to tiny Pearl, a gem of a bird.
May mothers everywhere be inspired by your nurturing heart.

Acknowledgements

I would like to give special thanks to my husband and the love of my life; I am grateful for all the labor and finances you invest in my beloved menagerie. You've been enormously gracious as you've listened to my on-going stories and revisions. Thanks for teaching me the rudimentary computer skills necessary to accomplish this adventure. Your support, encouragement, and computer skills have been indispensable.

To Sharon Hanson, my dear friend, surrogate sister and editor; I could not have developed as a writer without the example you have given me through your personal writing skills and manuscript procedures. You have cheered me on, believed in me and taught me. Because of your faith in me, I never doubted that I would accomplish the goal of a real book in print. I can't wait to write the next one.

To my parents, Bruce and Brenda Block, who suffered through my early years of animal collecting; I am so glad you taught me to love God's gentle creatures; my life is so much richer because of them. Thanks for teaching me to see God's blessings around me and for instilling the confidence within me to try new things without fear of failure. Mom, I learned to laugh at my mistakes and embarrassing moments because of your example. Life is full of those moments and if you can't laugh at yourself, it's easy to get discouraged. Thanks for that important tip.

To my closest friend, Debbie Allen; you've listened with great enthusiasm to all the details of my book, cheering me on and believing in me. Repeatedly urging me to hurry up and finish so you can read it. I appreciate the time you've spent listening to me brainstorm and polish wording on the on-going manuscript. It's great to have a cheer-leader.

To Ravena Dodds, who empowered me to try using a computer instead of handwriting my document; Boy! What a great new world that has opened up for me. Thanks for your help.

Also, special thanks to our former family physician, Dr. Henry Domke (now retired); You asked me to keep you posted about guinea fowl ownership. That request led me to record the details so I could keep that promise to you. Quite belatedly, I'll admit. Nonetheless, here is the promised information, preserved for your enjoyment.

I have the enormous joy and privilege of having a great many encouragers in my life, my church family, friends and family members who all believe in me. If I tried to mention each of you by name this book would be delayed for months. Each of you are equally important in my life and I treasure you. Thanks for standing behind me.

CONTENTS

Chapter 1   The Menagerie 1

Chapter 2   Be Careful Who You Follow............................ 11

Chapter 3   Dogs Don't Think Like People Do............................ 19

Chapter 4   Buffy's Big Lesson..27

Chapter 5   Growing Up is Complicated 35

Chapter 6   Live With a Purpose 49

Chapter 7   Love With All You've Got.............................57

Chapter 8   Gentle Leadership is Best.............................67

Chapter 9   Vanity, Vanity, All is Vanity.........................77

Chapter 10 Don't Grieve Too Long................................89

Chapter 11 Savor the Moment 99

Chapter 12 Today is Hatch Day.................................... 111

Chapter 13 Toddlers and Hatchlings............................125

CHAPTER 1
THE MENAGERIE

CHAPTER 1

THE MENAGERIE

My childhood sweetheart and I live, work and play together on about twenty acres of semi-wooded pastureland outside the small town of Mokane, Missouri, where we apparently thrive on hard work because we're always creating more of it to do. We're constantly improving the land, clearing timber and brush, seeding pasture, gardening, canning produce and maintaining the home place; in addition to all the tasks involved in caring for our multiple animals. In the thirty two-plus years of our marriage, animals have been a shared joy and the source of most of the work.

We have an ever-changing number of chickens and guinea fowl. Currently, two adult guineas, four adolescents and eight brand new hatchlings that Little Blue has just finished sitting on, three large laying hens, (New Hampshire Reds), two young white Silkie roosters, two young bantam hens, and one fiercely protective bantam hen with two brand new chicks. The animals are a source of constant amusement or consternation, depending on the moment in question.

Along with the birds we have four house dogs. Buffy is a nine-year-old Pit Bull terrier. She is the ultimate ambassador for the breed. She's gentle and nurturing with all adults and small children and lovingly attends to and protects our birds. Buffy is often in her doghouse on the porch with our birds all around her in harmonious companionship.

Casey is a very geriatric black and gray Pomeranian who totters around on arthritic legs surveying the goings on; barking from the sidelines at the activities of the others.

Tyras is our wild card dog. He's our six-year-old Boston terrier. He plays with and hassles Buffy regularly, keeping her active and irritated with his perpetual practical jokes and wrestling. Spike, our eight-year-old Chihuahua, is the instigator of barking and hysteria; he sets off the alarm then stands back quietly while the others whip the energy into a frenzy. This is most notable when we have guests arrive or if someone turns around in our driveway. This fact makes greeting our friends at the door much noisier than we would like. Our repeated attempts to quiet them have met with limited success. The most effective method we've found is to separate the dogs in kennels or rooms before our guests arrive. This keeps them from feeding off each other's energy.

Then there are the horses. Rogue is my husband's horse; he's a tall sixteen-plus hand (meaning over five-feet tall at his back) chestnut brown Appaloosa. He's sixteen years old and we've had him since he was four. He's calm, gentle and steady. He's a wonderful trail riding horse and a pleasure to be around. He forgets he's not a dog and can't get close enough to us for attention. He would come in the house and watch TV with us if we would let him.

Jefé (pronounced hef-ā, although my husband calls him Little Jeffee) is my personal riding horse. He's a nine-year-old Paso Fino. For those unfamiliar with the breed, Paso Fino's are a short, stout, Spanish, gaited breed; they "dance" instead of trot, making for a smooth, exciting ride. He's a rich dappled brown with a thick, wavy mane and tail that women envy and little girls long to braid.

Jefé loves to be handled and ridden, and has a friendly personality with an incredible sense of humor. I've never seen a horse with so much imagination. He picks up sticks with his mouth then wags them at the other horses to entice them to play tug of war. He'll poke them to irritate them with the stick until they bite it in frustration, then he tugs and they tug back till one of them lets go. They wheel around and buck or rear, nipping each other before they race off playing. Very soon they run back to repeat it all again. If his buddies don't feel like playing, he'll poke them in the hip with the stick until they can't resist him any longer and give in to join him for playtime. Jefé doesn't accept no for an answer. The other boys have learned it's easier to just give in than it is to resist.

One day I glanced out the window to see Rogue and Jefé standing face to face with lips nearly touching. As I watched, Rogue leaned back on his haunches, Jefé's face, and then all of Jefe's body was leaning forward; a mirror image of Rogue's movement. Rogue then leans forward, stretching as far as he can. Next, Jefé leans backward, slowly as though he's sitting down in slow motion. Rogue's body seems to stretch to follow the movement of Jefé's. Over and over they repeated this strange combination of movements. They repeated this unusual series as I continued to watch, mesmerized and perplexed. *What are they doing?* I wondered…

The intensity seemed to be building though the movement itself was small. Rogue leans forward, Jefé backwards. Jefé forward, Rogue backwards. They repeated this over and over again. After several minutes of watching, I was able to see a short length of stick between their lips. The stick had been hidden from my view inside their mouths, between their teeth with only an inch of length between them.

They had found a six or seven inch wooden stick, probably worn down through multiple play sessions. No doubt, Jefé had picked it up in his teeth and then enticed Rogue to bite onto it for tug time games. As I observed the stick games in the following days, I noted that they had found a new, longer stick to play with; the short stub had been retired. I found myself disappointed. It had been amusing to watch them play with the stub.

Jefé's half-brother Josey completes our trio. He's a glossy-black three-year-old Paso Fino. Josey is still in the training and growing phase, still angular and a little awkward. He hasn't been with us long but he's exceptionally willing and intelligent and we're anticipating great things from him. He is very social with people as well as his horse buddies and like Jefé, he's full of mischief and mayhem in the pasture. Everything goes in his mouth, like any toddler, so he has taken readily to the stick games. He promises to be an enthusiastic and tireless riding horse like his brother.

When our two sons were still at home (the older son is now a father of two tiny girls, and the younger, who's just finished college is pursuing a long range career) we didn't have so many animals, but without the boys I have a powerful need to nurture something!

So, then…

The fowl part of this story began because we live in Central Missouri, the unofficial tick capital of the world, and we are always open to creative ideas that might provide some relief from them. We adore animals and are happy for any excuse to experience a new variety. As with any new endeavor we start, my husband and I bought books so we could research the subject and equip ourselves for responsible caretaking. We found a delightfully informative book by Jeanette S. Ferguson called "Gardening with Guineas." She helped inspire us to tackle the challenge of training these crazy, amusing and noisy birds.

When my dad learned that we wanted to get Guineas, he said, "DON'T DO IT! THEY'RE SO LOUD!" He was emphatic in his warning, and I believe a little concerned for our sanity. In Dad's defense, I will say he had a point; they have definitely shown themselves to be boisterous. Many people refer to them as the farmer's watchdog. Nothing unusual happens near their territory without raising a raucous comment from the guinea crew!

We bought books, researched, plotted and planned to equip ourselves for bird ownership. We contemplated for a couple of years before plunging in with both feet. We don't do anything halfway, so this experience has been no exception. We've made the whole process as complicated as possible and blundered our way along. This was our first experience with birds of any type and guineas are a very wild bird, not nearly as domestic by nature as chickens. They are very independent, refusing to lay eggs inside the chicken coop, wanting to roost in trees instead of the chicken coop and generally speaking, desiring the opposite of whatever we want. If you want order, get chickens; chaotic amusement, get guineas. I like chaos, with a little order thrown in to keep me sane.

I have a friend that calls our wacky assortment of animals "The Cornwell Menagerie". The title is fitting; it's a sampler platter of breeds and types of animals. They create a visual kaleidoscope of shapes and sizes parading about the property for my amusement. I feel that each of them fills a unique role in my life and I can't imagine being without the joy any one of them provides to my days.

It's hard for me, at times to limit myself to a reasonable number of animals. My husband provides a necessary balance here. He provides the voice of reason to remind me that I have my hands full enough caring for our current number of animals without adding more.

It occurs to me at this point that some of you who don't know me well might be wondering: How in the world does she find the time to fuss with her animals that much? My answer? I don't work full time away from home. I clean houses, part-time for a few special clients who have become my friends as well, but the focus of my energy and the desire of my heart is caring for our family and our home. I work full-time at our home. I am happy in my work and run pell-mell towards the domestic chores that many run from. I enjoy gardening, canning produce, making our laundry detergent, baking granola and fresh bread and the many other chores involved in caring for our home in this lifestyle my husband and I have chosen.

Because I am at home, working on the various domestic endeavors here, I go outside quite often to pick fruits or vegetables from our small home orchard or garden, take care of the horses, feed or water the birds, mow the yard, hang laundry on the line or any other of the sundry duties involved in caring for our pets and home place. Some of the tasks vary by the season, but there is never a lack outside chores or activities.

Whenever I go outside or pass a window while in the house, I take a moment to enjoy the view. Our animals are my favorite part of the view. To my way of thinking, there's no point in having all these beautiful things around us if we don't ever pause to look at them.

One focus of my energy and time is our food supply. We care about eating healthy food. To this end, we grow and preserve through the process of canning, freezing or dehydrating fruits and vegetables.

Many of the things we preserve are grown by us, others are given to us by generous friends with a surplus. The chickens play a role here, too, through supplying eggs. No, in case you're wondering, we don't eat our chickens. We do buy butchered chickens from a local, organic farmer who does all the hard work of butchering and plucking. (I do have a limit to what I desire to do.) We buy raw cow's milk from the same farmer. Sometimes we churn the cream to make our own butter. Fresh ice cream is also very worthy when made with fresh farm milk! We buy butchered lamb, farm-raised hog and Angus beef, too. It takes time to research, hunt down, retrieve and cook in the wholesome way we want to eat, but it is worth the effort for our health.

Whenever our friends have bumper crop produce years and they fear that things will go to waste, they call me. I'm well known for my canning compulsion. For example, one year I canned approximately seven-hundred and-twenty jars of food, in addition to freezing numerous pounds of cherries, berries and various vegetables, and dehydrating anything that wouldn't fit in a jar or the well-stocked freezer.

We look forward to heavy fruit crop years. We have a two-man system, my husband and I, for making fresh pressed apple cider. What a treat! We dive into bushels and bushels of apples, washing, chopping, pressing and canning them for days at a time. What fun we have working together and then enjoying the fruits of our labor later.

We work very hard, taking care of our material blessings, but we play too. We lead a full and happy life. One of the things we enjoy is riding the horses together on trail-rides in our local area. We frequently load them into our horse trailer for a ride on Mark Twain National Forest land trails about thirty miles away from home. I'll pack our saddlebags with a lunch to enjoy on one of the bluffs that overlook creeks or valleys within the park. It's so refreshing to exercise our bodies and relax together as we admire some of God's blessings to us. Mark

Twain is a beautiful, rocky, rugged place with bluffs and creeks within its forested borders. Though we have traveled to other places farther away, we have seldom seen beauty that rivals what we can enjoy so close to home.

We both enjoy teaching Bible study classes. I teach a twice-monthly in our home to a half-dozen ladies. We are both involved in the ministries of a small, local church where my husband teaches the adult Sunday school class, along with preaching at our church on occasion, as well as other churches when called upon.

Besides caring for and interacting with the animals, I dabble in numerous other hobbies and interests; in jewelry making; sewing, furniture repair and upholstering, and doing whatever else might need to be tackled. My life is rich and full, I'm doing all I've ever wanted to do.

CHAPTER 2

BE CAREFUL WHO YOU FOLLOW

CHAPTER 2

BE CAREFUL WHO
YOU FOLLOW

I had told a local horseback-riding buddy of our plan to get guineas. She had toyed with the same idea and beat us to it by ordering twenty-five newly hatched guinea chicks, called keets. Hatcheries require a minimum order of twenty-five keets so they can huddle together during shipping to generate the necessary body heat to keep them alive. My friend didn't need twenty-five, so she offered to split the order with us.

The hatchery notified my friend a few days before the keets were to arrive in the mail. This gave me a few days to prepare the nursery for the babies. I put the rabbit hutch purchased for bird nurturing inside the garage so I can pop out to check on them often. I can hardly wait for them to arrive!

They're here. Yippee! The post office called at 7:00 a.m. to say they had arrived. My friend and I hurried down to pick them up. They are adorable! All I hoped for! I didn't know what to expect they would look like, but I'm not disappointed. As you may be detecting, I'm all about the journey and process involved in pet care. My husband refers to my style of process as 'making a production out of it.' I enjoy learning and experiencing new things on nearly any subject, but I dive in even more enthusiastically if there are animals involved.

They came in a small cardboard box, similar in size to a shoebox. The hatcheries send keets out just as soon as they dry after hatching. They aren't given food or water during shipping, but because of God's perfect design, the yolk of the egg sustains them in these first hours of life, just as it did during their development inside the eggshell. I always assumed that the yolk was the soon-to-be chick or keet, but it is actually the food source for the developing bird. The little speck inside the white of an egg is what will become the tiny bird.

Guinea keets are very colorful when they first hatch. They are colored with an earthy tapestry of brown, black, white, tan and gray. As is true of many birds, guineas do not begin their lives with the body color they will have as adults. Adult guineas come in several colors; the most common is called pearl. Contrary to the name, a pearl does not resemble the gem; it is not a whitish iridescent. In guinea fowl, the color pearl consists of a predominantly dark gray background, splashed over the top with white polka dots. It looks as though the bird has been splatter-painted. Lavender color is similar to pearl with the difference being a background color of soft dove-gray, creating a nearly lavender appearance. A lavender guinea appears solid colored from a distance, but is polka-dotted on closer inspection. Their image is delicate and lovely. Chocolate color is a rich cocoa brown without the polka dots: mocha-like. I have heard that there are numerous other colors, most of which I haven't had an opportunity to see.

Guinea fowl are comical in appearance. They sport a pear-shaped, bottom heavy appearance; they remind me of a gourd with legs. They have skinny legs that seem unsuited to the task of supporting the mass that rests on them. The speed and grace of movement they display are unexpected given their structure; they look as though their legs would just collapse under the weight they support. On the contrary, they have strong legs and move very swiftly with agility. Guineas are fast runners and can also fly very well; both facts they demonstrate enthusiastically if you need to catch them.

Guineas have fuzz covered heads as babies, but at maturity have bald heads with funny hair-like wisps sticking up at odd angles. They also grow strange pointed, bony protrusions called helmets on the tops of their heads. A guinea's head shape is similar to that of a vulture. Not very attractive in my opinion, but effective in hiding them from predators when moving through tall grass. The variety of guinea I'm describing is called the helmeted guinea and is the most commonly seen variety. The males have larger helmets than the females. The males also develop larger wattles than the females. Wattles are the dangly, fleshy parts that hang at the sides of the guinea's face, much like a chicken has. A male guinea's wattles dangle farther and cup under more than a female's do. This is one of the main ways to tell the sexes apart.

Guineas grow to weigh about three to three and a half pounds at maturity. They are a very hearty bird, quite tolerant of most weather conditions. They pant when it's hot, seeking shade and breeze to cool themselves. Given opportunity to choose, guineas go out of their confinement to brave the elements. They prefer fresh air and room to run. Freezing rain, heat, mud; none of these things daunt them. They are not fans of snow and will sometimes stay inside working up the nerve to walk out in it. In a rush of pushing, shoving and flying they burst forth from the chicken coop door. Yelling and screaming in revulsion as their feet touch the cold substance.

Many people allow their guineas to roost wherever they choose when it is time to sleep, but I don't want to take any chances with the wildlife I know might enjoy eating my guineas as a snack. I intend to teach them to roost in our soon-to-be-constructed guinea house.

I chose to purchase hatchlings instead of older birds because I learned through my research that guineas are creatures of habit. If they have grown accustomed to living in a certain place they will not take well to being relocated to a new home. A guinea should be confined in the location you want it to sleep for several weeks before being released from confinement or it will run away to return to its former home.

In discussions with our locals at the country store gathering spot, I have heard many stories of guinea ownership. One man, I was told, bought a whole flock of adult guineas from a distant neighbor. As soon as he got home with the birds, he released them to explore their new home. To his surprise and horror, his brand new birds raced and flew away as quickly as they could move.

The next day, he called the former owner to lament the loss and was told that they had returned to him mere hours after being released. This scenario repeated itself several times in the days and weeks that followed. Many of the guineas became casualties to the road or predators on the subsequent journeys back home. No one could tell me whether the new owner gave up trying to contain them or if they finally decided to stay at his farm, but I got the message loud and clear: if I want to keep my birds at home, following my rules, I must train them from keets. Sounds simple enough, I feel sure I can handle it.

The tiny keets arrived and I put them in the rabbit hutch in the garage with a heat lamp, chick starter crumbles, and water. I check them frequently all day, attending to their needs. I have to teach them how to drink. To accomplish this feat, I have to hold them upside down and dip their little beaks in water to let them taste the water. This is a little tricky without totally dunking the little darlings. When hatched and taught by their mothers, they learn by their example, but in lieu of a mother, they have me. When my husband comes home from work, eager to meet the new keets, we see them milling around aimlessly, peeping and seeming hungry with no idea of what to do about it. My husband taps his finger rhythmically in their food to simulate pecking.

One bright baby has an 'aha moment' and starts pecking at the food. The others stampede over en masse and peck greedily at their chick starter. Thankfully, guineas are tremendous copy-cats, so once one gets the idea, the trend catches on.

The first night, our thirteen little puffballs attempt a mass suicide in the water fountain. The fountain is a gallon-size container with a moat-like trough surrounding it. I went to check on them and found six or eight of the babies stretched out face down, beak to toe in the trough of the water fountain. It is as though one little show-off had said, "Look what I can do!" and dove in belly-flop style, then the rest had felt compelled to follow suit. We're back to the previously stated fact that guineas are copy-cats. In this instance, it was not in their best interest. Peer pressure happens even in the bird world, I see.

I fish most of them out alive, but two are successful in their desire for death. I dry the live ones with a hair dryer and put them back in the rabbit hutch with their heat lamp. Hours later, I return to discover that in my absence they've tried it again; lost another one. Keets are not very bright! The term 'stupid birds' is coming to mind. I gather up some decorative pebbles I have on hand and put them in the water trough to prevent the keets from going diving again; though they can still drink between the pebbles without any more dangerous diving activities occurring. After a week or two we remove the pebbles when the babies have matured a bit and all danger of drowning has past. *Good Grief*!!!

Within a few days, the keets start getting feathers to replace their fuzz. The feathers look so out of place; one here, one there, starting with the tips of the wings and sprouting rapidly all over their bodies, almost before my very eyes. I'm finding that birds mature faster than any other animals I've observed. From the time I make my last check on them before I head off to bed to the first look in the morning, they have visibly grown and changed.

It is a somewhat wistful feeling for me, I love baby animals! Although I'm aware that adulthood and maturity is the end goal, I really relish the baby stage with all animals. I thrive on the perpetual drama and the need for problem solving and adapting to their changing needs. I love care-taking and nurturing even when it becomes overwhelming.

I especially love puppies. Periodically I get puppy fever, when this hits me I find it helpful to go visit puppies that are not of a breed I long to own, lest I fall victim to the desire to take one home. I find that if I can hold and play with a puppy (or better yet, a whole litter!) for a few minutes, then the moment will pass and I can move on, thankful for my own well trained adult dogs. I've heard people say that the bad thing about puppies is that they become dogs. I understand what they mean; I think I'll miss bird babyhood when it's over too.

CHAPTER 3

DOGS DON'T THINK LIKE PEOPLE DO

DOGS DON'T THINK
LIKE PEOPLE DO

Well, despite all our plotting and planning, we found ourselves ill-prepared. Our guineas were growing like weeds but we had no house for them. The race was on to build it before they outgrew their rabbit hutch. Between the surviving ten fast-growing adolescents, a feeder, a waterer and roosting sticks for guinea gymnastics, it was getting a little tight in their hutch.

My husband scrambled and researched again; finally designing a little A-frame house on stilts with a wire floor. We needed both the stilts and the wire floor so the birds' waste material could fall through

and drop to the ground for us to clean-up and re-use as fertilizer in our garden. We also designed the house to have a little bird-size door with a birdie ramp on one end for entering and exiting. The opposite end would have stacked nesting boxes equipped with lift-up doors on the outside for egg gathering. One slanted side was to have a two-foot square door for reaching in to feed and water the birds and we would wire in a light switch, and hang their feeder from the rafters. An old bunk bed ladder was to be propped against the wall near the bird door for roosting and sleeping. The other slanted side would be vented to prevent them from overheating in our hot and humid Missouri weather.

We gathered materials and went frantically to work.

We also needed to prepare our fast growing birds for the big outside world which included our dogs. To accomplish this, we gathered the youngsters into a wire cage, put the cage in a gardening wagon and took them outside with us while we built their house. The dogs were able to watch the birds and get used to seeing them move while they flitted about in their wire cage. We could correct the dogs for any excessive exuberance and the birds were safely out of reach while performing their "meet and greet." We would roll the babies out each day in their wagon to join us as we worked and roll them in when we were done. They loved playing outside in the fresh air and grew even faster, it seemed. The day came when the house was nearly done. Nothing left but the big door. We were so excited that we decided to put them in their new house right away, inside their wire cage before adding the door the next day.

Hours later, after preparing to leave for church where my husband was guest-preaching the evening service, we went out together to check on the babies so that we could give the longed-for guinea report to the congregation. We were appalled to see Casey, the arthritic Pomeranian, tottering back and forth under the wire flooring scattering frantic babies within their cage confines. Tyras the Boston terrier was outside the birds' house looking on as Casey chased. We looked inside the door opening to find five of our beloved babies lying dead in their wire cage. As nearly as we could determine, Tyras had performed a maneuver that terriers are prone to do; a mighty leap through the door opening. He had apparently clawed through the wire of the cage, overcome with great curiosity and a desire to play with the babies. (We both assumed and agreed that his motives were not malevolent; but the result was no less disastrous.) The annihilation left us bereft and appalled.

What a betrayal. We had taught our dogs to be kinder; these were family members, after all. We hurriedly chewed-out both Tyras and Casey, cleaned-up the mess, gathered the remaining babies back into the safety of the rabbit hutch to protect them until we could properly attach a permanent door—and with heavy hearts hurried to church to tell a much less cheery guinea report than we usually delivered.

The guinea report often consisted of happy little illustrations of Biblical principles observed while watching the guineas grow and learn. The illustration this time was not a happy one. It went a little like this: Dogs don't think like people do; we can't expect them to feel human compassion.

Another lesson was learned from this: Our electronic dog fence needed to be moved so our dogs couldn't reach the birds' house. We also determined to install some wire around the legs of the house to keep other animals from getting underneath it. Another lesson learned the hard way, as usual.

We found very early, through these and other lessons, that there is a lot to raising guineas. This is especially true if you're blending them with dogs that haven't been around birds. This fact continued to play out at odd and unexpected times when we thought we had nothing but bliss and harmony between dog and fowl.

The next instance came soon after the first one, after we decided to get some bantam chicks. I figured if you're going to have birds running around, they may as well be cute birds! Banties are the answer to cute! I had six little banties that had matured to the stage where they were just starting to confidently come and go from the chicken house. The dogs were watching them from a safe distance, due to their invisible fence boundary. (It's buried underground, but their collars beep at them to warn them they are nearing their boundary lines. If they don't heed the beep, they get a shock. It's very effective.)

I had taken Casey's collar off of him overnight, but had forgotten to replace it in the morning. This allowed him to enter the 'birdie safe zone.' The quick, darting movements of the chicks had him enthralled; he was moved with curiosity and dove into the midst of them, killing three of my new bantie youngsters. Though I was not there to see him in action, I had seen his fixation from a distance before. None of the other dogs could reach them and Casey was near the chicken house when I found this carnage. Thus, the deduction; and I was flabbergasted! Who would have ever thought of a Pomeranian as predatory? A cat, perhaps, but a lap dog? Surely not!

Over the course of the first year of bird ownership, we had a few more mishaps. Buffy the Pit Bull and Tyras the Boston terrier would occasionally start rough housing with each other when an unfortunate chicken, never a guinea for some reason, would wander by and they would turn their attention to the bird instead. We lost several in this manner.

We tried various methods of correction to discourage them from harming our chickens. We would lay the dogs on their back and put a live bird on top of them to show the birds' dominance in the pack hierarchy; we flopped the dead birds all over their faces and bodies in hopes they would be frightened of them next time (this method is called flogging); we ostracized, shouted at and swatted—all to no long-term benefit, that is until the day we employed an old wives' tale remedy. It was extreme, but extreme problems call for extreme solutions.

CHAPTER 4

BUFFY'S BIG LESSON

CHAPTER 4

BUFFY'S BIG LESSON

To back up for just a moment, let me explain the thought process that went into our decision. We had invested an exorbitant amount of money, effort and emotion into our birds and dogs. We wanted to keep both groups safe. It is not acceptable behavior for a farm dog to kill stock. Farm dogs that kill stock are often killed by angry neighbors or owners. We love our dogs enough to give them a chance to rehabilitate, but we cannot accept killing. What to do?

Our choices seemed to be:

1) Give away our offending dogs to bird-less homes.
2) Get rid of all birds.
3) Put dogs to sleep. Most farmers would do this one, but their terminology would be to put the dogs down.
4) Try the wives' tale we'd heard was an effective method to stop the senseless killing of innocent birds.

We chose method four. As stated previously it was extreme, but it was imperative we resolve this problem. Here is the story of the last straw that initiated the final decision of which option to choose.

A friend had brought her grandchildren over for a visit one lovely summer day. After a tour of the animal kingdom outside, we retired to the house. We were discussing how beautiful the birds were as well as how sweet and gentle our dear Buffy was. (We call Buffy our Pit bull Ambassador because she is so gentle to humans as well as to other dogs. She has changed the perceptions of many individuals about her breed.)

Meanwhile, Buffy was alone in the yard while we visited inside, the other dogs being inside with me and my guests. A sweet bantie hen had passed in front of Buffy. I'll never know what possessed our gentle "ambassador" at that moment, for when we exited the house to enjoy one more glance at the pretty banties, instead of beauty, our eyes were accosted by the vision of Buffy lying on the ground with one of my tiny beauties lying across her front paws, lifeless. My friend's grandchildren were horrified by the image before us. My friend and I tried to comfort them and I bid them goodbye while muttering assurances. "Buffy's a sweet dog, really she is. I can't imagine why she did this. Dogs just don't think like we do."

Buffy didn't bite or tear the hen. She didn't want to eat it. She just killed it. There wasn't a mark on the bird; she had apparently shaken it, breaking her neck. That was E-NOUGH!! I decided this was going to stop once and for all! It was time to implement the old wives' tale we'd been told was the last ditch cure for chicken killers. (It pains me to call her that dreadful name. I feel like a traitor. She did the deed however, so the name applies.)

I marched into the house, got kitchen shears, marched to the garage for wire and marched back to a very sheepish Buffy. I proceeded to flog her with the dead chicken while yelling at her in a somewhat tearful frenzy. "Bad dog! Bad dog! Bad girl!" Buffy simply disintegrates under disapproval; I hated to tell her she was bad. To say the words "bad girl" to her is akin to tearing out her heart. I promptly cut off the chicken's leg and wired it to the back of her collar, where she couldn't reach it. The concept here was to let the chicken leg rot and stink so she would be repulsed by the odor and reminded not to kill chickens again. She could not remove the leg nor could she get any satisfaction from chewing on it. Because she could smell it but not reach it, her frustration level must have been unbearable.

She was stuck with it. It was July and over ninety degrees with heavy humidity in Missouri that year, so it didn't take long for her to want that chicken leg to go away. The smell was only part of the punishment, however. Buffy is a house-dog, so she was also ostracized, kept away from our family life, put outside, alone. Just her and the stinky, rotting burden on her neck.

The other dogs shunned her as though they wanted nothing to do with the reeking stench that emanated from her or the disapproval that emanated from us towards her. Casey our stuck-up Pomeranian flounced his fluffy skirt and sniffed at her in haughty disapproval as he passed near her. Tyras bullied her, growled and body-checked her on the way by. He seemed to be taunting her, "You got in trouble. Ha-ha! It wasn't me this time." Spike the Chihuahua avoided her like the plague he seemed to think she was. And Buffy? She hung her head in apparent shame, slinking around dejectedly.

As time passed, Buffy moped and pined in deep shame and humiliation. She started to get growly back when Tyras taunted her. She wasn't eating well. We were concerned about her emotional well-being. The training process lasted for a very long-seeming week, during which time she turned her head from any bird that passed her way, walking in a sideways posture that gave them a wide berth. She seemed to understand the concept that birds were the reason for her current heartache and that she had better stay away from them.

My husband and I surmised that if the lesson hadn't been learned by now, it probably couldn't be learned. It was time to stop her exile and return her to her indoor home and family. We undertook the two-man job to clean her up. What a stinky, messy process it was to remove the wretched stench from her. I can hardly find words to describe just how BAD she smelled. I will spare you the gory details of that odor. Suffice it to say, I didn't eat chicken for some time after that myself. YUCK!!!

After throwing away the slimy, offensive collar, we held her at arm's length to spray her with the garden hose. The whole disgusting, labor-intensive job was performed outside in the fresh air. Many lather-rinse-repeat cycles were necessary to have her pass the sniff test that would gain her entrance back into our home. When the intensive production was finally complete, we brought her back into her normal, family life. Her punishment was over. She sighed contentedly, curling up on the couch, from which she hardly moved for the next twenty-four hours. A hard lesson which we hoped Buffy had truly learned from.

We found as time went on that she had learned her lesson well, and as our dog-pack's leader, she apparently had taught the lesson to the other dogs as well. Our extreme method was a success. It's been three years without another killing from any of the dogs.

We have learned from our experience with owning multiple dogs at the same time, that one member of the pack is usually the initiator of the energy in a given situation. If you can change the energy driving the initiator, the problem will often resolve itself. Buffy was apparently the initiator of chicken death. (Or at least she could control the energy within the pack as it related to chicken death.) Now the dogs and the birds move in and out of each other's groups in our yard without such disruptions.

Ah, harmony at last!

CHAPTER 5

GROWING UP IS COMPLICATED

CHAPTER 5

GROWING UP IS COMPLICATED

Behind our compact red chicken house stands a thirty-five foot cedar tree. It has a wide spreading canopy of limbs. My husband has trimmed the low hanging ones from the base to allow clearance for our tractor when he brush-hogs the pasture for weed control. This also allows us a lovely, clear view of what our animals are doing in the field surrounding the tree. This tree is the favorite resort spot for our horses and birds alike. We often look out to see the horses standing under its shady branches with chickens and guineas dust-bathing at their feet. The guineas are sometimes enticed by the allure of its branches swaying in the breeze. On such evenings, they decide to "camp out" for the night and roost in those lovely branches.

Tonight is one of those nights. Papa is refusing to go to bed in the coop. All the other birds have gone into the house without my encouragement. Papa is insisting on a night of solitude in the open air. He's resisting my calls. I have trained the guineas to come when called in case they need to be moved away from something I don't want them to do. My call consists of "Bird-e-e-s" in an extended sing-song while shaking a can of wild bird seed to lure them. This method has proven very effective at retrieving them from the road, the roof of our house, our newly planted grass seed or wherever I don't want them to be. When they come to me they are always rewarded with a sprinkle of birdseed.

I've shaken the bird seed can till my arm hurts and called "BIRDIEES" till I feel silly, but he's not coming. He is staunchly resisting my pleas to go to the safety of the coop. He's our last adult male, and we just lost a guinea last night under this very tree. He obviously doesn't grasp the gravity of the situation!! My concern is rising to near panic as dusk is fast approaching. There is a very short window of time to convince a guinea to move if it has already chosen a spot to roost for the night. We learned this fact when our guineas were youngsters and they would play outside enjoying the last rays of daylight; suddenly screaming in confusion because they couldn't see well enough to find their way to the chicken house twenty feet away. They are blind as bats when the light is dim. They mill about, running into things in blind terror until we come out as a team; one in front, calling to them with a flashlight in hand beaming to show them the way and the other walking behind them, arms outstretched, herding them to the ramp of their safe home.

Armed with this knowledge, I know I have to move fast to convince him that it is not a wise night for camping out. I'm searching the ground for something to toss at him to startle him down out of the tree. My eyes fall on a stout two foot long stick. It seems to have enough heft to sail all the way up to where Papa is roosting twenty or so feet from me. I grab up the stick and heave it in Papa's general direction in an attempt to coax him to the ground. I succeed in scaring him higher up into the tree instead. I give up hope of moving him and walk away praying he makes it through the night.

This morning I hurried out to find poor Papa down from the tree, hobbling about on a crooked, mangled foot. In an attempt to hit something near him in the tree, I had instead struck the dear bird with enough force to break a bone. His outside supporting toe is obviously broken. It is dangling out to the side at an awkward angle not supporting anything. He hops around on his one good foot, intermittently setting the bad foot down to test the pain level. His long-term outcome doesn't look promising. I fear my gentle protection has maimed him for life!

Gazella is our only remaining adult female, so if she and Papa want guinea companionship, they are stuck with each other. Personally, I would hate to be stuck with Gazella; she is not the epitome of sweetness. She is not a natural born encourager. Gazella is taking note of Papa's injury and showing uncharacteristic sympathy for him. Guineas as with most birds, are not known for compassion for their own wounded; often picking at or even killing the weak, sick or injured.

Papa's foot hurts him a lot and he needs to rest often. They sit together under the shade of various trees as they move slowly, Gazella gracefully walking and Papa limping and hopping around eating ticks and other bugs in our yard. Guineas are seldom still, so resting is not natural for them. They are intense about their bug-eating duties; break times are generally very short. Gazella has been kind and attentive for two days, waiting patiently as he slowly hobbles along with her. All at once it seems she's abruptly tired of his whining and is deciding to end it. Permanently! With no warning at all, Gazella just snaps; erupting into intense bird-violence.

I'm watching in horror as she chases him, hobbling on his poor mangled foot. She tackles him, viciously pecking, pulling out huge beakfulls of feathers. Her head is covered with his blood and his back has been plucked by her till it is naked and raw. They're flying into tree branches and running under vehicles as she relentlessly follows his evasive efforts to escape her wrath. I've been following them, darting in front of their frantic scramble, trying to distract her from her brutal quest. Gazella is not about to be distracted. She's very single-minded in her determination. This takes the term hen-pecked to a whole new level.

In a rush of well-intentioned concern, I grab my trusty fishing net to take after Papa with a loving hysteria of my own. Fearing for his life, I'm certain that the only way to save him from Gazella is to isolate him away from her to heal. With maniacal fervor and incoordination, I dart all over the yard, scrambling after him, wielding my net, missing as I scoop at him, falling down to my knees, face first in the mud, pursuing him as he is dodging Gazella's attacks as well as mine. Poor Papa is terrified; all the women in his life are out to get him.

Finally, he's distracted or exhausted enough to pause for a moment. I fall upon him with the net and capture him, wrestling him in my arms, within the net, squawking, struggling and screaming as we proceed to the safety of the barn. As I walk to the barn, I reflect on how relieved I am that he wasn't further injured by my bumbling efforts to save him.

Once there, after untangling him from the net, I plunk him in the rabbit hutch we reserve for raising young birds, or in this case; hospital stays. I bustle around, gathering up food and water to place inside with him. When I open the top to place it inside; out he flies in an attempt to escape confinement. He flies up to roost on a barn rafter. He has already showed me he isn't receptive to my suggestions about where to roost, so I think I'll just leave him there. I put the food and water on the barn floor for him and close the door to keep Gazella outside till he recovers and she forgets about killing him.

Several days later I release Papa from his hospital stay. Gazella has indeed forgotten her desire to murder him. They seem to have fallen into a wary truce, though it is not cuddly by any means. Guineas mate for life, and it is becoming apparent that they are not each other's life mate. Papa is guarded in her presence and the feathers on his back are ratty and tattered for weeks; a visible reminder that she is not to be trusted.

Meanwhile, we are also raising another group of keets. We are nearing the end of the six week long process of raising them to the point of being placed in general population with the big kids in the chicken house. The next step is placing them in a wire cage within the coop so the adult birds can get to know them without any harm coming to the keets in the process. After a week of the birds getting to know each other through the wire, I open the cage's door, a drop down ramp that is similar in style to the one they will soon use to enter and exit the coop. They hop in and out, enjoying the freedom, and run back to the safety of the cage whenever they feel insecure.

The keets still don't venture out of the chicken house for another week, until the morning that one brave keet flies the coop, literally. He looks back in alarm as he realizes that he's – gulp – ALONE; none of his buddies followed him. The little fella is panicky, frantic and confused about how to return to the great indoors and safety of his cage. The terrified baby is running back and forth, under the ramp, clueless that it is the very means of return to his flock.

The keet has rammed into the wire that surrounds the coop's legs, accidentally wiggling his way between the wire squares to end up underneath the house gazing longingly at the safety and friends above it. Screaming in adolescent panic, he jumps straight up to repeatedly bang his dopey head on the wire floor above as his fellow keets answer his wails from the unattainable safety just inches away from him.

Now the silly youngster is in a literal world of poo. Due to the nature of the wire floor's purpose, there are bird droppings everywhere that he is scrambling around in as he tries to escape. I am not amused. Guess who will have to rescue the little dope? Yep, you guessed it, me.

I'm removing the staples that anchor the wire to frame of the coop, pulling back the wire on each end and trying to chase him out. The little rascal is avoiding my efforts to help him. I've run back into the house to get a large trash bag to lie on the filthy ground. I'm on my belly on the trash bag, equipped with my fishing net and a duct-taped handle extension to give me a bit more reach under the coop. I'm groping around, wallowing in the poo, attempting to retrieve the incompetent fowl. After MUCH ado, I finally manage to catch the ungrateful twerp. I put him back with his buddies and everyone, except me who is now in desperate need of a shower, is happy about the reunion. I hope tomorrow goes more smoothly. Each day is a new experience with youngsters.

As I open the door for the birds this morning, the brave keet promptly shows all the other keets how to race down the ramp and through the wire to join him in poo world. I'm considering putting food and water under the coop and just letting them live under there till they find their own way out. Drats, I can't do that. I might be reported for bird abuse. I need a new plan.

I must change the wire that surrounds the legs of the coop to prevent this happening every stinking day till they get the hang of the ramp. If the keets are able to repeat this maneuver it will become a daily habit. I'm not okay with that possibility at all. I apparently need to cover the larger wire with smaller wire as well. As I contemplate the wire repair job I perform bird gathering duties, another job which requires no small amount of finesse.

First I set about gathering the necessary tools to gather the keets. Fish net with duct-taped handle extension. Check. Pliers. Check. Wire cutters. Check. Wire cage. Check. Chicken wire. Check. Oh yes, trash bag and gloves. Check. I take a deep breath; it's time to wade in.

I once again remove the wire surrounding the legs of the coop, I crawl around as the babies run just beyond the net's handle extension, repeatedly, I might add. Finally, after many failed attempts and a lot of stinky poo slinging, one less coordinated individual is trapped in the net. I carry the unhappy keet over, within the net's tangled grasp to deposit it into the cage. Thankfully, when the rest of the keets hear its cries, they run to the cage to reunite with it in the fresh air. I stealthily sneak up on them, and then pounce with my net, trying not to flatten them in the process. I scoop them up, one or two at a time, to deposit them through the flip top opening in the cage. Sometimes, as I place one in, another will hop out. This is exasperating! After fifteen long minutes I have accomplished my goal, at last. I must prevent future misadventures.

I go through the grueling process of the chicken wire installation job, alone, my husband is at work in order to pay for all the fun I get to have at home. I stretch chicken wire over the square wire anchoring them both to the legs of the coop. I'm making sure to leave a way to access the manure for composting. Even after installing the double wire barrier, all of my bird wrangling problems are not over yet. I have blocked the keets from their head-banging and poo-wallowing activities, but they still can't seem to figure out how to maneuver the walk up the ramp. They run 'round and 'round the house, directly under the ramp, absolutely clueless that it is the answer they are searching for.

But the happy day arrived eventually. Two brilliant babies have finally figured out how to ascend the ramp. I feel like blowing a trumpet and throwing a party in celebration! I'd been netting them for over a week using the aforementioned method and I'm sick of it, so this is great news! As I'd mentioned before, guineas are great followers, so now they will learn from each other.

Well, although it's not AS difficult as previous days, I still need to net some of them and place them partway up the ramp, nudging them to ascend the remainder of the way on their own. This exhausting process is lasting yet another two weeks, with less and less stragglers as time wears on. I come in hot and sweaty after the evening birdie round-up and exclaim to my husband, "I hate this stage!" Instead of feeling relaxed and ready for bed, I feel keyed up, adrenaline surging, temper sometimes flaring, feeling like I need a sedative. Instead I choose to laugh with my husband as we recall that this too shall pass; it's just one stage of the journey.

Finally, Papa can't stand watching my inept bumbling any longer and in mercy steps in to rescue me in training the kids. Hallelujah!! I need a break! Papa is eagerly embracing the role of father. He's leading the youngsters up and down the ramp. Glory, what a beautiful sight!!

They parade all over the property as he gives them the tour. Now they are exploring the sand-filled round pen we use for horse-training. They are using it for sand bathing. They all flop down to roll in the sand to clean their feathers of dirt and bugs. It reminds me of a mass pig wallow. The guineas stretch out on their sides, dragging along, scooting, kicking and rolling. They come up shaking big dust clouds of excess sand, making their own miniature sand storm. Sand is apparently a great exfoliant because they sure look clean and sparkly and seem quite refreshed. I assume it's similar to how we humans feel about a refreshing shower.

Papa and the babies are often gathered around the mirror that Gazella loves so. The youngsters stand back from it at first, stretching their necks, leaning forward on tippy-toes to peek at their reflections in curiosity. They quickly warm to the idea when nothing jumps out of the mirror to attack them. They are fascinated and peck at their reflections in the mirror.

The kids trust Papa; he is a kind, patient leader. Gazella and Papa are not closely sharing in the parenting duties, though each of them has a role to play in their raising. Papa teaches them the hands-on practical life skills. Gazella enforces any necessary discipline while following behind at a distance.

The previous relationship issues between her and Papa have definitely caused a rift in their friendship. Gazella has become the black sheep of their guinea family. She is allowed to attend family gatherings, but is not really an accepted member of the group.

As the weeks have passed, Papa seems to have forgiven her for trying to kill him and they have merged closer as a family unit. The keets are starting to choose partners and lay eggs. What a crazy sight. The mating races are a riotous event. Two male guineas will set their sights on a pretty young female and attempt to show her which of them is the best suitor. They accomplish this through foot races. The suitors charge across the yard with wings arched up and chests pushed out like adolescent males of the human persuasion are also known to do when showing off for a girl. "Look at me," they seem to say to her as they run. Then they turn on a dime and change positions, the lead male in the rear. They have been going at this for hours now. Every time I pass a window, I see a flurry of activity as they race by. Once the female determines the winner, they mate for life.

Guineas are very discreet in their mating practices. In the four years we have owned them, I have only witnessed one mating event. Chickens are not private at all, so this discretion surprises me, I wouldn't have thought there would be such a difference between chickens and guineas.

Our young guineas, like youngsters of any species, are dealing with the normal pressures of growing up. Asking internal questions like: *Who should my friends be? If my friends go out to play in the road, should I follow them? If my friends dive into the water fountain, should I dive in too?* And similar ponderings.

One day as they pondered life's complexities, a young wild turkey wandered into the yard. It was an adolescent male, looking for a mate perhaps. He had probably shown interest in young females within his own flock. The resident tom turkey may have been displeased with his overtures towards "his" ladies and thrown him out. Not knowing much about wild turkey life, I can only speculate.

Apparently the adolescent male turkey was musing on the same questions that my birds were thinking on and he desired answers too. His ears were drawn to the sounds of our guineas and being all alone, he came to see if he could join their flock. They met him with a friendly air and invited him to join them for the day's activities.

There are some similarities in the appearances of guineas and turkeys; they both have dark gray striped and mottled feathers in their wings, the main body color of the typical guinea's dark gray is common to both birds, they are similar in shape and profile, and from a distance it's easy to mistake them. In fact, I have looked out our bedroom window to see turkeys in our pasture and momentarily mistaken them for my guineas. Perhaps there are additional similarities that I can't detect. I'm unfamiliar with most of the vocalizations of a turkey; they may sound like guineas. The young turkey seemed to think so. The birds all seemed able to overlook the differences between them; deeming them insignificant as they enjoyed each other's company.

Something happened to demonstrate this when I had a lady come to purchase a saddle I had for sale. We were exchanging pleasantries, walking around the yard on the way to the barn to look at the saddle. She was admiring our place and land when she burst out excitedly, "Wow, I wish I had my shotgun! I've got a clear shot at those turkeys in your yard." I said, "I'm glad you don't. Those are my GUINEAS!" I have some serious concerns about her carrying a shotgun, especially after her boast that she's a dead-on shot at what she's aiming for. I hope she identifies her target better than that when the lead starts to fly!

The young turkey followed our domestic birds all over our yard. To their water container, their outside feeder, to the chicken house, but not inside it, onto the patio, the sidewalk in front, everywhere they went, the turkey followed. Our birds talked with him and allowed him to follow with them; but only at a distance of eight or ten feet. At times he would try to ease in closer, just to be rebuffed by them and moved away again. He seemed a bit flustered by their standoffishness. "Can't we all just be friends?" he seemed to say.

As the day wore on, he became more aggressive, arching his wings and charging them. This is dominance behavior; he was probably trying to establish a spot of leadership within the group. He really wanted to be accepted by them. All youngsters want a place to belong. They spent the whole day together from early morning to gathering dark forging a tenuous friendship.

My husband and I were curious as to what would happen when night fell. Would the turkey join them in the chicken coop? Would the guineas follow him out into the woods? Would we ever see the turkey again? It had been such a strange occurrence, we had no idea what to expect. When night fell, I was relieved to find my guineas safely tucked in their own house.

If our tame birds had chosen to follow him to the woods, they would have been in danger. His wild ways though alluring might have met them with tragedy. The young turkey had learned from the first moments of his life how to watch for signs of danger. Our birds had been coddled and protected which made them more vulnerable to the dangers beyond our protection. They had a false sense of security about things around them. Even birds need to choose their friends carefully lest their life choices bring them harm.

The young turkey came back to visit for several following days, but when none of the guineas would follow him away, unable to entice a suitor; he lost interest. We never saw him again after that. Perhaps he found a flock of his own with others of his own kind: after all, birds of a feather should flock together.

CHAPTER 6

LIVE WITH A PURPOSE

CHAPTER 6

LIVE WITH A PURPOSE

Pearl is the sweetest bird I have owned so far. She's very delicate in both color and stature. She weighs all of about a pound. She's a Belgian Bearded D'Uccle bantam chicken. D'Uccles are known as a breed for being gentle, friendly birds. They are often chosen for 4-H showing due to their diminutive size that is wonderful for children to handle. Their delicate beauty is irresistible as well.

D'Uccles commonly come in two colors, the porcelain, which Pearl is, has a pearlescent near white background color with soft, dove-gray highlights and gentle cream low-lights, all covered with a luminous iridescence. The mille fleur color is a rusty, chestnut background color with black outlines on the wing and tail feathers accompanied by splashes of white and black spots on their body. Mille fleur color is, in my opinion, gorgeous and my personal favorite of the two. There are other colors too: black, white, black mille fleur, self-blue, lemon, buff mottled, blue mille fleur and numerous others. Sounds like a lovely assortment; I'll take one of each, please.

Pearl has a sweet nature and loves attention. She adores my company, seeking my companionship more than the company of her bird friends. Upon catching sight of me, she comes running to greet me with a low clucking tone, begging to be held. She squats down low and waits for me to pick her up. When I place her back on the ground after holding her, she follows me around on fluffy feathered clown feet. A tiny comb and floofy cheeks that look like a walrus mustache complete her ensemble. The combination of features is adorably comical. I find it impossible to contain my laughter as I watch her.

Many evenings I amble out to the chicken house to sit in its doorway watching and listening to the birds as they settle in for the night. I enjoy the peaceful hum-tweet noises of the guineas and the clucking noises of the chickens. It is a relaxing and refreshing vacation-for-the-moment type experience.

One such evening I am sitting in the chicken house doorway watching them when little Pearl jumps up next to me gently demanding attention. I put her in my lap where she stretches out on her little tummy, legs straight out behind her and closes her eyes to sleep. I stroke her bunny-soft feathers and hold her quietly for a few minutes before putting her down. Before I can crawl out of the doorway, she is up on the ledge, perched beside me, making her own special low clucking sounds, looking up at me, begging for more. Who could say no to that? Not me, I'm powerless against such sweetness! We repeat this process several times until, finally I have to just put her down and ignore her pleas for more.

Pearl is what is known as a broody hen. That means that she has an intense desire to incubate eggs. Most hens don't even consider setting on eggs until they've laid six or eight of them, but tiny Pearl clutches every single egg to her with single-minded purpose. When I gather eggs every day I need to reach under her to find the ones she is hoarding. She hoards all the hens' eggs, not just her own. She hides them from me, clasped in her little feet beneath her where I have to pry them out of her grasp. If you allow hens to 'go broody' or set on eggs, they quit laying, so since we didn't need more babies, but do want eggs, I continue to take to take them away.

Apparently, Pearl is tired of me constantly stealing her precious eggs, so she's started hiding them from me. This has become a larger problem than just being deprived of the use of her eggs for cooking. She doesn't want to leave her eggs unprotected, which means that she won't be locked up and protected overnight either. Predators are most likely to attack her at night, so I don't want her out overnight.

I need to implement a new strategy that changes from day to day. Keep the barn door shut so Pearl can't get inside to lay her eggs in the haystack, check under the hosta plants for eggs, block the window ledge under the deck so she can't nest there either, check under the bean tower in the garden where she laid them yesterday, etc. It is a daily job to keep Pearl safe.

Tonight at near dark, I close the chicken house door for the night. Little Miss Pearl is nowhere to be found. I call and call for her. She nearly always comes to the sound of my voice, but, alas, no Pearl. I am starting to get tearful. I begin praying: *Lord, the Bible tells us your eye is on the sparrow, so I know you care about all the birds. You've displayed your love for me through animals many times so I know you care about this. Thank you for the special gift of Little Pearl. You know where she is; please show me. Amen.*

I went in the house to ask my husband to help me find her. We grab flashlights and hurry out into the now dark night to search for her. As we exit the house, we no more than walk out the door when my husband looks down and says, "Here she is!" She had heard the sound of my voice and came to the patio by the back door to wait for me.

Just like the song says, "His eye is on the sparrow" and in this case the chicken. He cares about all the birds! But, in this instance I feel he demonstrated that he cares about me!

Little Pearl and I continue our egg-gathering conflict for several more weeks after that night until one night in mid-November when she doesn't come to the chicken house at bedtime. I call her but she doesn't come. I search but can't find her. I worry all night and into the next day. Still no sign of my sweet little Pearl. My husband and I hunt high and low.

My husband has been saying for some time that he's worried about how I will handle it if anything bad ever happens to Miss Pearl; so he searches with me fervently. After scouring every spot we can think of, we find her tiny body safely nestled between hay bales in the barn, and there are thirteen miniature eggs beneath her. She has been sneaking out to the barn to stash them for a couple of weeks.

We scoop up Pearl and her little eggs and remove three of them so she can easily and safely cover the ten that remain. We place her and the eggs in a nesting box in the chicken house. This will allow her to safely pursue the motherhood she so obviously longs for and refuses to be dissuaded from.

From what I've heard and read, chicken eggs take twenty-one days to hatch under normal conditions. 'Normal' is usually warm spring or summer. I have never heard of a hen hatching eggs successfully in winter, so it is a gamble. It would also be a gamble if I didn't let her keep some eggs to nurture. She will continue to evade my egg-gathering attempts by finding better hiding places; putting her in great danger to do so. Nurturing is in her nature and she simply must sit on some eggs! Okay baby, I hear you, you win.

Now my sweet Pearl doesn't seem at all concerned that winter is the wrong time for egg hatching. She has been desperately trying to accomplish this very task for months, despite my best attempts to stop her. Motherhood is her goal and the only way to make her happy is to let her have a try at it. Given the weather conditions, we are certain she can't possibly succeed, but at least she'll be safe in her snug little nesting box while she makes her valiant attempt.

CHAPTER 7

LOVE WITH ALL YOU'VE GOT

CHAPTER 7

LOVE WITH ALL YOU'VE GOT

Pearl settled in contentedly on her eggs; no more conflict between us. She sat quietly and determinedly on her little clutch day after day. Setting sweetly nestled in her own little cubby with her beloved treasures. She was still very happy to have me pet her but no longer wanted to be held; she had work to do and was not about to be taken away from it.

She was a fastidious caretaker of those eggs! Each morning when I opened the door to the chicken house to let the birds out for the day, she would race down the ramp to run outside and use the outhouse facilities. She would not even relieve herself inside the chicken house for fear she would contaminate her eggs. She would quickly get a drink and eat a little bite, dashing back to her nest. She was determined not to let those eggs cool.

If the eggs cooled they wouldn't hatch; somehow God has instilled this knowledge within birds. During warmer seasons a bird has about twenty minutes before the outside temperatures will affect the eggs hatchability, but Pearl was dealing with cold temperatures for her hatch. This meant that she had to be very diligent indeed.

This ritual continued for almost three weeks. I peek in to check on her and find tiny eggs spilling out from under her. I fear she is losing interest and not being careful, so I poke them back under her. To my surprise, as I poke beneath her, I find five full size eggs under her as well.

The big hens had hastily deposited them in her nest while she was out on break. Each day I find, it's necessary to remove the big eggs, which Pearl seems relieved to have me do; she is then able to fully cover her own little treasures.

Well, it's been twenty-six days since setting began; all the books say chickens should hatch in twenty-one days. I've almost given up all hope of a hatch. I'm planning on taking her eggs away before we have a "bad egg" explosion; I'll wait until tomorrow.

Brrr, it's a frigid nine degrees this morning; I'm all bundled up in my insulated coveralls, prepared to do morning chores. The first step is to let out the birds and check on Pearl. As I open the door, much to my delight, I'm greeted by the sight of Pearl standing with six healthy little black chicks. Each one of them is popping their unbelievably tiny heads out from under their protective momma to see me. Despite my lack of faith in her, Pearl has successfully hatched seven of her ten eggs. That would be a good hatch rate in the summer. It is nothing short of miraculous in the cold dead of winter. There's one tiny, dead chick as well. It probably got chilled after exiting its shell before it dried off. There seems to be one egg that wasn't fertile and didn't hatch. She had managed to shield her new hatchlings beneath her warm body as they each emerged from their shells all wet and vulnerable. To have protected them from the bitter cold as they dried was an amazing feat for a first time mother. What a special surprise. I never expected the hatch could be successful.

The chicks are about the size and weight of a cotton ball with legs. Each one of them is solid black; not at all what I anticipated considering their mama's porcelain color and daddy Furbee's solid white coloration. I have learned the initial colors on chicks don't indicate the color they will have at maturity. This will be interesting to watch. *What colors will we end up with, I wonder?*

I quickly moved Pearl and her chicks to the rabbit hutch in the barn with a heat lamp to assist Pearl in her efforts to keep everyone warm. I sincerely doubted the babies could survive another night in the nine degree winter weather in the unheated chicken coop. It was so terribly cold.

I had obviously underestimated Pearl's tenacity and mothering abilities. There was no reason to fear for her children. She takes to mothering like a duck to water and acts like an old pro. One would never suspect she's a first-time mama.

It is darling to see her with her little black fuzz-balls. Out in the barn when checking on them, I find her gently hovering over their delicate bodies. When they hear the sound of my approach, six tiny little black heads appear between her wings and body or beneath her fluffy breast feathers, curiously watching me. It almost seems that her chicks are heartier than the chicks I've purchased from feed stores, they are downright robust.

Her tiny chicks grow quickly under her attentive care as she teaches them how to eat and drink. She has a special vocal tone for each activity. She gathers them in a group for mealtime and for water breaks. She completes the whole parade-like event in a matter of one or two minutes. Food first, hurry kids, hurry: now a drink. Quickly, Quickly! She growls a distinct harsher tone when urging them to hurry. She seems to understand that they are in danger of freezing if she isn't extremely careful with them. She then hurries them back to the heat lamp. Pearl stretches up on tippy toes to give them room, hiking up her feathered skirt to allow them access to the warm canopy of her body heat. As she lifts her little body up for them, Pearl urges them with her vocal tones, advising them to make haste. In this case, every moment is truly a matter of life or death.

It is unusually cold for Missouri this December and it's difficult to keep their water thawed even though we have a heat lamp on for them. It is just bitter! I marvel every day at her care of them. How does she do it? I've never seen any mother of any species take such tender care of her children.

One day when her chicks were close to a month old and too large to all completely fit under her petite body, we had a ground fault breaker trip in the barn. This caused the life sustaining heat lamp to go off. My husband and I enter the barn to discover the problem. We find a frantic little Pearl. She is clucking and making agitated sounds. Her body is laid flat, wings spread as far as she can reach, trying desperately to cover her chicks to keep them warm. It is a heartwarming sight to see our tiny Pearl giving all she has for her little kids. Her babies are no longer as vulnerable as they were when they were younger, but Pearl is still just as protective as ever.

It is a scene my husband and I will never forget. I wouldn't have believed birds were capable of so much emotion and concern. Her devotion is breathtaking. What love!

We of course, move quickly to reset the breaker and ensure their warmth and safety. It took Pearl a few minutes to calm down and feel reassured that the danger had past, but she finally let the kids crawl back out from under her body's protection.

Each day finds the chicks showing a higher activity level. They run about within the rabbit hutch; playing and jumping like children do. No longer always sheltered under their mama's breast at all times; they move about individually to eat and get drinks. Lining up in single file comes to an end. They are also developing individual coloration. One has a lovely cream colored ruff round his neck and splashes of rust, burgundy and deep green are coming through. This must be a rooster since they are always more flashy. Another has a rusty ruff around her neck with a fluffy "bouffant hairdo" with no other flashy colors; a hen I presume. Yet another hen with a tan ruff and matching hairdo. Another is a slightly less colorful bird with deep russet on its black body background and erratic bits of blue, green, tan and red tones. There is a virtual smorgasbord of colors in this bonus winter hatch. All chicks are predominantly black with additional color shades upon them. Furbee, it would appear, has a recessive gene for black with wild color variation as well. Who would have thought that a plain white daddy would produce this beautiful parade of colors?

Finally, in about mid-January, weather conditions have warmed up a bit. By now, the babies are fully feathered. They have nearly out-grown the rabbit hutch and are weaned from their heat lamp; spending less and less time under their devoted mama. It seems to be time to move them out to the chicken house. All of this is guesswork on our part. This is our first experience with personally overseeing a hen hatching her eggs. This, our first experience, is a puzzler. The books don't talk about this scenario. This hatching event is NOT normal; even for a hen-hatch.

Our only previous experience has involved the rabbit hutch and heat lamp method I have previously described, which included pre-hatched chicks purchased from the feed store. Even under normal conditions and more favorable weather, chicks still have to be kept under a heat lamp, even in the warmth of summer with a nearly constant ninety degrees until they are fully covered with feathers. Considering the cold conditions, this fiasco should not have worked. But Pearl is an extraordinary mother hen; so work it did.

We moved Pearl and her toddlers out to the chicken house, in with the general population of fowl. The other birds didn't even seem interested in the new kids as Pearl showed them the ropes. A few more weeks pass with Pearl and the babies never venturing out of the door to explore the outside world. Protective Pearl refuses to go out without them and they're too timid to even poke their heads out in curiosity for several weeks. The babies are now nearing three months old.

Finally one day, the chicks peek out and file down the ramp to see what is beyond the bird house. Pearl stays with them as they go out and trains them about staying close to the house for safety from the unknown dangers in the big outside world. She also demonstrates how to find their way back up the ramp for bird feed and water throughout the day. Most importantly, she shows them how to return for bed-time just before night fall so they will be safe from predators.

Two weeks pass and Pearl is leaving her youngsters to spend their days alone while she rejoins the rest of the adult flock in their daily travels around the yard. The chicks still cram themselves around her in the nesting box at bed-time (maybe they still enjoy bed-time stories). They have grown very self-sufficient in their personal care, so she seems to feel confident to leave them on their own during the day time.

By now it is early spring and Pearl has started laying eggs again. She had stopped laying eggs all through the setting, hatching and nurturing phases. She seems ready for a fresh round of mothering. She and I are back to our former relationship of her asking to be held by me. I also find myself once again performing the unpleasant task of scouring high and low to find out where she has stashed her eggs to hide them from my attempts to gather them.

The dreaded day has inevitably arrived; Pearl hasn't returned for birdie bed-time and in spite of the best efforts my husband and I put forth, we can't find her. Days and months pass with no clue to her whereabouts.

Eventually, months later, when working together in the barn to rearrange hay, my husband and I find her tiny, lifeless body. It's nestled between hay bales, in a miniature, nest-sized hollow she had sought out and claimed for a nursery. She is still sitting on a nest of her precious eggs. She'd gone there to take another chance on motherhood. A predator, probably an opossum, had killed her from beneath and just left her body, otherwise undisturbed, still sitting on her treasured eggs. My husband and I looked at each other and said in unison, "Pearl died doing what she loved."

I feel that there's a lot that can be learned from her example. She has shown how to love with all you've got; with no holding back. Pearl made a giant effort, despite all odds, and gave of herself to others unselfishly with no concern for the personal price she might need to pay.

The feeling of loss that came from losing Pearl and other losses in life have helped to teach me how to feel joy more deeply when it comes. Without occasional pain I seem to grow numb to just how rich my life truly is. It's a bit like our younger son said when I picked some fresh strawberries from our garden to give him. I warned him that a few might be tart. He replied, "The sour ones help you appreciate just how sweet the sweet ones are." Pearl was one of the sweet ones. She was a rare gift and I would gladly choose to go through the pain of losing her again just to experience the wonder of watching her priceless life.

Pearl's children have continued to bring joy as she had done. We kept two adorable hens from the hatch and named them Polly and Anna. (They are the "bouffant girls.") They came by their names because my husband refers to me as Pollyanna (after the Disney movie about a young girl who always sees the bright side of a situation). Polly and Anna are good hens. They lay eggs regularly and tend them carefully. Polly recently hatched her own brood and we found she's even broodier than Pearl was. Polly's possessive of all eggs in her vicinity. No matter who they belong to; whether guinea or chicken. She continues her mama's legacy of motherhood, though not so sweetly. I can expect a violent pecking of my hand if I approach any eggs she's set her sights on. She doesn't desire my interference into her egg-centered world. "Don't touch me, I'm busy," is her mantra. No stroking or holding dear Polly. I miss my sweet gentle Pearl.

We've found special homes for the rest of the chicks from Pearl's hatch. My closest friend and her husband took one rooster we named Oliver. He's brilliantly colorful: black, emerald-green, burgundy, cream and rust colors explode upon his body's tapestry. He's a watchful, gentle rooster with his flock of a couple dozen hens. We temporarily kept one rooster for ourselves; we dubbed him Sparky. He is flashy colored, a trait passed on genetically from his solid white father, Furbee, who ironically always throws black bodies with splashes of lots of other brighter colors too, and sweet-natured like his mama. We eventually passed him on to a friend who admired him while visiting us. Sparky enjoys being held by his owner as he watches television in the living room each day. We don't often hear reports about the others, but we trust that their lives have also been observed and enjoyed.

CHAPTER 8

GENTLE LEADERSHIP IS BEST

CHAPTER 8

GENTLE LEADERSHIP IS BEST

Our first experience with roosters spoiled us. Our rooster Furbee is a prince with impeccable character (for a bird). He demonstrates you don't have to be big or mean to be the leader. He's a white Silkie breed bantam chicken, weighing in at about two pounds. He has a wild looking punk rocker "feather doo" on his head and it naturally flops when he struts. He's fluffy with heavily feathered feet and a gentle disposition. He's a quiet, considerate leader for the girls. He treats his ladies with respect and dignity, calling them to himself when he finds a tasty morsel to eat. He never eats the special treats; they're reserved for his sweeties. He unselfishly waits till they are through eating before he will eat anything himself. He leads his flock around the property, growling in alarm to warn them if he sees a hawk or any other sign of danger.

Whenever Furbee wants some romantic time with one of his girls, he does a special little dance for her. He kicks one feathered foot out sideways while moving in a circle around his intended. There's a "snap-snap, snap" noise when he does this. He bobs his head while stretching and fanning one wing towards the kicking foot. All of this is his elaborate attempt to woo her and ask for her permission to mate. A receptive hen will stop and squat in submission to him. His girls love him and he encounters very little resistance to his advances.

Many roosters are known for their rough treatment of their hens. I've heard numerous stories of hens with bloody backs and sparse feathers due to the insatiable drive of their roosters. Some people buy special "clothes" to protect the backs of their hens from rooster spurs. They're called aprons, sort of a leather armor to guard against a rooster's voracious handling when mating. No need for such apparel with sweet, gentle Furbee. He's a kind, considerate breeder of his flock. His girls adore him and happily follow him all around our acreage.

We had a large, vibrantly colored rooster during Furbee's early reign as Rooster King. He was blue-black on his main body with a rust colored neck ruff resplendent with emerald green splashes on the tips of each neck feather, and emerald green on his long tail plumage and wing tips. We called him The Pretty Rooster, and it was an understatement. The Pretty Rooster wanted Furbee to share some of the hens with him. Furbee was not a fan of that plan, so they had frequent disagreements on this subject.

Furbee had an unusual facial feature which became problematic around that time. His comb was not the usual "stand up" type that most roosters are adorned with. He had a rounded, fleshy comb that looked like a tiny brain sitting on his forehead. This was not a deformity; it is a unique feature of his breed, but it sure looks funny. Well, it became the focus of The Pretty Rooster's wrath. He relentlessly attacked Furbee with both feet and spurs flying into his body, beating him violently with his wings as Furbee tried to defend himself against his much bigger bird rival. The Pretty Rooster pecked and pecked and pecked at Furbee's "brain comb" till it bled profusely.

From my kitchen window I witnessed the on-going trauma that The Pretty Rooster was inflicting on Furbee. Clearly, Furbee was losing ground, showing signs of being tired out by the fray. He tucked his bloody head under his own wing to protect it from further damage in the passionate skirmish. Like a weary boxer, clinging all the while to The Pretty Rooster to prevent him from getting leverage to further peck and pound at him. Poor valiant Furbee! Seeing crimson blood dripping from tiny Furbee's brilliant white feathers was too much for my mother's heart to bear. I rushed out with my every-ready fish net and scooped him up. I put him in the rabbit hutch to recover. Thankfully, his wounds were more superficial than the violent onslaught would have indicated.

I kept Furbee in the barn a few days, safe in the rabbit hutch. My hope was that a little time apart would distract the boys from their hormone driven conflict. Furbee's brain comb healed quickly so I put him on the outside ground with the thought that his first thought would be to find his flock. Twenty steps into his quest he ran into The Pretty Rooster and started the whole messy business again. This time I netted The Pretty Rooster instead and into the rabbit hutch he went. It was obvious that the boys weren't going to give up the fight; one of them would have to go to a new home, or die from the intensity of their conflict. So I made a call to a local farm that sells eggs. They had forty hens and only two roosters. The Pretty Rooster was very welcome there. He settled in nicely; a group of eight hens chose him right away and followed him like a willing harem. He had his own girls with no protest, and Furbee was the king pin in our flock once more.

Furbee never challenged me or showed any dominance or aggression to any humans. It was easy to assume that most roosters are that agreeable because he was so pleasant to be around.

We enjoyed the peace of Furbee's reign as king for almost four years. Then one misty spring night we went out to close the birds in for the night and found an explosion of feathers all around the coop and surrounding area. To our dismay and sorrow we discovered six tiny bodies littered about. From what we could determine, some strange dogs had killed our banties for sport. They left the big chickens and guineas alone. The only body we couldn't find was sweet Furbee; we found his feathers but that was all.

The flock was lost without him, their gentle but mighty leader. The hens wandered around, scattered and aimless. In their search for leadership, their gaze fell upon Buffy, our Pit Bull terrier. They were already comfortable with Buffy because they spent time in the flowerbeds at the front of our house or on the front porch near her doghouse, sharing her food and water. Buffy was a reliable, steady landmark in their world.

By the second day after the Bantie Massacre, we watched Buffy walk down the front sidewalk followed by the comical-sounding slap-slap-slap of chicken feet as the hens waddled along behind her everywhere she went. Down the walk, to the driveway for some bird seed, (which Buffy would also partake in, side by side with her hens), towards the barn, wherever Buffy's yard patrol took her, they went too. This unusual relationship continued for weeks until finally our oldest hen, named Big Red, emerged as their fill-in leader.

I hurried to find a new Silkie bantam rooster to lead our brood of girls. I ended up with two instead of one rooster, so I could determine which will be the best personality to emerge. One of them my husband pronounced as "New Furbee." He looks beautiful, bright, new and improved. The other I named Benny. They came from a breeder of show birds and New Furbee is a looker: so soft, fluffy and snow white. He has deep raspberry purple combs and wattles and lots of plumage. Benny is fluffy and sweet, but not a stunner in the looks department. They are four or five months old, but not yet mature. The girls accept their presence, but don't seem to realize they're boys.

The shocking day came when New Furbee crowed. The girls physically jerked to attention and you could almost hear them shout in unison: "A MAN!" They are elated and start to follow him from this day on.

New Furbee may have appeared to be new and improved at first sight, but his temperament is not remotely similar to our former Furbee. The more mature he becomes the more he struts and I've begun to hear a furtive rustling noise behind me as I walk across the yard from the coop each morning. I'll turn to see New Furbee close behind me, abruptly stopping and feigning interest in the ground whenever I look at him. He follows me, skulking, furtively haunting my steps. Over time, despite my forceful movements to claim dominance, his sneaky behavior escalates. He's progressed from from stalking me to jumping at my ankles. His white feathered neck-ruff standing on end looking like wispy dandelion puffs in his aggressive pose. He attempts to claw at my ankles and he pecks at me violently.

This behavior is unacceptable. *I will not have it! I will not be dominated by a two-pound rooster, thank you.*

I initiate his retraining program promptly, with moderate sideway shoves, using my foot. This incenses him; he comes back with fervor. Another shove, more returned vehemence. *Oh, my!* I didn't know he could jump THAT high. *Ouch!* That hurt, now my leg is sore. New Furbee won that round.

Next day, stick in hand, I walk toward him to move him out of my space. *He's unimpressed; up comes the dandelion ruff. He's jumping at me again. Poke him with stick, try not to run. Oh, dear. This is truly embarrassing. I can control a thousand pound horse with decent proficiency but I am bested by a tiny rooster with a Napoleon complex!*

The events that followed are being recorded for the accuracy of the tale, not out of pride in my behavior. I ask you in advance; don't judge unless you've experienced similar rooster mayhem.

I learned to beware of sneaky New Furbee, waiting behind a bush to flog my legs, so I wore boots and carried a large stick everywhere I went on our property. When New Furbee approached aggressively I smartly gave him a whack to cause him to retreat. Sometimes it took five or six whacks. In the beginning of our war, I felt deep remorse for this tiny bird and his obviously inadequate brainpower. *Just give up and we can stop this,* I thought. However, as time goes on my remorse is turning to ire, as I can't enjoy my own yard for fear of a rooster attack. I've resorted to kicking (with only enough connection with his torso to send him tumbling, uninjured). And to chasing, yelling, and the occasional yelp and retreat maneuver when his aggression becomes too much for me. There are moments of fragile truce between us when New Furbee shows temporary deference to human authority. However, he continues to revert to former ways. Two or three embarrassingly long months drag on in this manner.

What to do?

I was pondering the dilemma as I walked out to check the birds when closing them in for the night, I found New Furbee inside huddling under the coop's low hanging feeder, hunched down, obviously trying to hide from something. He was covered with blood, his comb torn and dangling. I glanced around to determine the cause of his injury and found "gentle" Benny blinking innocently. He seemed to have Furbee's blood all over his beak and throat. I don't know what New Furbee had said to Benny, but it had been the last straw in Benny's book. He had put New Furbee in his place as only another rooster can.

Ironically, Benny and New Furbee have always snuggled together when they sleep at night, and that night was no different. As soon as New Furbee crawled out from under the safety of the feeder, Benny sauntered up to him and cuddled up, intending to sleep. The whole conflict was over for him. No hard feelings, he seemed to think.

New Furbee's whole demeanor is transformed. He's just a shadow of his former cocky self. That was the end of all aggression towards me or Benny. I haven't seen any more conflict between them. Benny lets New Furbee tag along behind the group, a part of the flock, but in a position of respect for Benny's leadership. They cuddle together at night as formerly, and New Furbee's comb and plumage have healed. It has been a long humbling journey of self-discovery for him; he doesn't seem to shine as brightly or walk with his previous panache. It seems he's learned that he isn't the center of the universe.

CHAPTER 9

VANITY, VANITY, ALL IS VANITY

CHAPTER 9

VANITY, VANITY, ALL IS VANITY

Gazella is our matron guinea hen. She's been with us since our first group of hatchlings four years ago. She bristles about with a bossy, domineering attitude and a hard, glaring facial expression. Whenever there is a squabble amongst the birds, Gazella is sure to have started it. She is empirical and selfish. No matter how many piles of wild bird seed, the favorite treat of all our birds, I stage about, she chases everyone else away to hog it all for herself. She pushes, shoves, and bullies everywhere she goes. She's a cross between an old school marm with ruler in hand ready to smack for any infraction, and a drill sergeant enforcing marching orders.

Gazella loves to watch herself in a mirror. We have one resting against the outside of our coop for just this purpose. When I walk out early in the morning to release the birds to roam for the day, Gazella pushes her way through the crowd to emerge through the coop door first. She immediately hurries to her mirror to start each day with a glimpse of her own perfect reflection. She stays for hours, gazing at herself. Thus her name: Gazella. She stands there looking, cooing dreamily, and tipping her head from side to side. Talking and talking to herself, until her legs get tired. Then she sits down and continues to drink in the view of her beauty.

Gazella laid a nestful of eggs in the chicken coop and she's shown intermittent interest in setting on them. She'll quietly sit on her eggs in the coop hour after hour, until a look of alarm passes across her face. Abruptly she'll jump up, running to the exit ramp and her mirror. There, of course, she'll again become distracted by her own beauty, forgetting any thoughts of her eggs.

When closing the birds in tonight, I remove Gazella's beloved mirror. My hope is that she might, without its distraction, focus on motherhood exclusively. When morning comes, she shoves her way expectantly down the ramp to the spot her mirror should be. She squawks in alarm, setting up the most hideous caterwauling imaginable. She shrieks and runs around the coop to see if her cherished mirror is hiding on the other side. So much for not being distracted. Ten minutes of wailing and grieving later; I relent, admitting defeat; and return her mirror. She never does hatch those eggs.

Gazella puts on an air of self-sufficiency, but underneath the façade is a neediness she seldom allows us to see. For example, she has stretches of anxiety that may last several days or longer wherein she waits for me to close her into the chicken house after dark. The normal evening consists of all the birds, chicken and guinea alike finding their own way to bed with me following along later to close the door for them once they're inside. I have tried numerous times to push my luck by going out earlier than true dark, but the birds don't want to waste a moment of daylight. They refuse to go to bed any earlier; so, after dark it is.

For some reason unknown to me, during these anxious spurts, Gazella refuses to go to bed without me being physically present for the event. On these unusual nights she calls to me from the sweet gum tree behind our deck. If I don't respond to her, she'll come to the front door to yell. She then moves back to the deck rail peeking in the kitchen window, hollering for attention, proceeding to the outside furniture by the living room, peeking in and pecking on windows to illicit a response from me. I emerge from the back door to do her bidding, and she comes running, obviously pleased to see me. She turns on her heels to follow me excitedly to the chicken coop. All of this activity occurs BEFORE dark, changing the normal routine. She likes to keep our relationship fresh and remind me who's in charge, I suppose.

I am perplexed by her behavior. I'm certain she's not afraid of the dark, nor is she confused about how to walk up the entrance ramp, since she's been successfully entering by herself almost every night for four years. I believe she simply desires the security derived from seeing me come out the door to tuck her in bed with a bedtime snack of wild birdseed.

Once we have walked together across the yard, Gazella scampers up the ramp and hops quietly into the house with her fowl friends. Well, quietly for her anyway. She pushes, shoves, pecks and jostles her way through the door. All the other birds are already sleepy and peaceful. It takes a few minutes for the energy to calm down when Gazella comes on any scene. My husband and I ponder her bristly personality and come to the conclusion that though unpleasant to her buddies, her toughness helps her survive, and thus, has merit. The most pleasant, docile birds are most susceptible to predators, due to their submissive personalities. They squat down in submission when frightened making them prime candidates for being nabbed. Gazella's wary, suspicious; *"Just who you think you're messing with?"* attitude makes her less approachable as prey. She's the only bird we've kept safe for the whole four year duration since we began this journey with fowl.

Months pass with Gazella's continued fixation on the mirror. She'll snatch a quick glance before joining the other guineas for the day's activities; much like we ladies grab a look in the mirror and pat our hair or adjust our clothes while racing out the door in the morning. Other days she seems to clear her complete schedule for a whole day of "me time". As I look around the yard, counting heads to check on the birds I come up one short. "Where is Gazella?" With her mirror. Again.

As the weeks and months passed, the mirror's appearance becomes more and more weathered looking. First, the backing comes loose from the wooden frame due to rains. Next, the wooden frame itself dangles dejectedly on one end then the next until all the sides are missing. Gazella is undaunted by the mirror's bedraggled appearance; it still performs the vital function of displaying her splendor. A strong wind knocks it down, breaking off a corner. We prop it up, and she carries on her love affair with her image within its now broken reflection. A near tornadic wind flung her mirror out into the pasture. The horses stepped on it out of curiosity about its shininess, shattering it beyond all usefulness.

Gazella is in a quandary. Where does a girl go to look at herself in this one-mirror town? Her wondering gaze falls upon my husband's one-ton Ford truck's shiny, reflective wheels and big chrome bumpers. OOH PRETTY!! It is love. Now, anytime we can't locate her we know just where to look. She and her truck are inseparable; it has become her new obsession. She squawks in resentment at my husband's impertinence if he dares to drive off with it, after all, in her mind, it is Her truck.

The truck has some mechanical issues and my husband needs to work on it. He pops the hood and crawls up on the bumper to investigate the problem. Gazella calls the whole guinea gang over to shout at him for his intrusion into her own private party. The cacophony becomes deafening as it reverberates off the hood. He shouts to me above the roar, "Call off your birds, before I kill them!" I run to the rescue, shaking the wild bird seed container, calling them to follow me to the chicken coop to eat, leaving him to work in peace.

With this method, I'm creating a flock of spoiled brats. By using the training tool of wild bird seed in a shaker, I'm conditioning the birds to come when I call them. In turn the birds are learning how to train me as well. Whenever the garage door is open they enter the garage and congregate around the container of bird seed, demanding a snack. I don't want them in the garage because they leave messy droppings in their wake. I move rapidly to dispense their seed, outside the garage. Whenever either my husband or I drive in the driveway, all the guineas and chickens come running, they recognize our vehicles and come to escort us up the drive. Dropping whatever they were doing, they come straight to our car and then directly to the coveted bird seed container. They storm the garage, denying them seed is almost impossible because they stand in the way of the garage door preventing us from closing it. It's just easier to give it to them and move on. It's alternately endearing and annoying in turn. Birds are smarter than I ever imagined them to be and are full of comical and unexpected antics. My husband and I chuckle frequently as we watch them.

One other event also displayed the intelligence of the guinea fowl, contrary to the opinions we frequently hear from others. For some reason the birds were choosing to camp out in the cedar tree in lieu of the coop, much to my dismay. No amount of coaxing or calling with bird seed would lure them in. One morning during this rebellion, as I made my way towards the coop, the guineas raced to meet me, squawking vehemently. It was then I noted the scattered pile of the feathers underneath the tree. Undoubtedly, the group had witnessed the decimation of one of their own. When night came I made my normal trip to the coop to lock the chickens in. I was delighted to see all the guineas within the safe haven of their coop. They were able to reason the cause and effect of their previous actions, and realize the enclosure of the coop would provide them with protection. Problem solved. Well, for now...

In the fall and winter months my routine includes letting the birds out first, then proceeding to the barn to feed the horses. I always have an expectant entourage as I move from the coop to the barn. The birds waddle, run, and in the case of the guineas, fly to the barn to help me feed the horses.

It should be noted; guineas are good at flying, unlike chickens who seldom do more than a hop with small air clearance and some ineffectual wing flapping to resemble flight. Guineas fly often; to get up into trees for roosting, to get on our roof (not a sanctioned activity!), or to avoid things on the ground that they don't want their feet to touch. Their flying skills are similar to turkeys; they can fly for several hundred feet at a stretch before needing to land on something to rest.

Rogue's feed trough is the favored zone, the birds push and peck at one another for the right to hover near him because he's a messy eater. The birds can hardly contain themselves as they wait for the showers of grain to fall to the ground. They eat well too as they mingle under the horses' feet; unheeded while horses contentedly munch their food. This is a peaceful example of barnyard co-existence, all enjoying the grain together. Nothing is wasted in this harmonious, natural form of recycling.

The first snowfall in a young guinea's life is traumatic. Guineas are desert birds from Africa originally, so snow is not welcomed by them. The first snowfall is met with squawks of alarm and revulsion. As soon as their feet encounter the cold snow, they take off in flight, gliding through the air across our yard to land, still squawking onto the horse's backs in order to avoid landing in the cold, white stuff. The horses are accustom to the guineas' presence and are unbothered by the intrusion.

One of the most humorous things I observe the guineas doing involves our garden. My husband installed a double-strand electric fence four inches above ground level to keep our chickens out of the garden produce. Our garden consists of a series of twenty, four foot by eight foot raised wooden beds, approximately eight inches in height. Guineas, I have discovered, are polite gardeners, seldom injuring plants or swiping our food, content to eat the bugs on the plants instead. This is not the case for chickens. They scratch, unearthing young plants and stealing any food goodies they can find. The guineas are resourceful enough to find a way around the fence barrier in order to pursue their bug-feasting inside the garden. They hop high enough to take a small flight over the fence to go in, once inside they work industriously to remove weed seeds, squash bugs, white flies, grubs and various other pests. We are thankful to have them help with the work.

When the guineas have finished their garden chores, the raised beds make a nice launch pad for the guinea exit. They stand behind each other in a single file line on top of the landscape timbers. One by one the creative thinkers hop over the electric fence, shock-free, waiting for their turn like fidgety kindergarteners. The waiting becomes too much for those in the back of the line causing them to impatiently fly up to exit out of turn. I've witnessed them employing this method numerous times. I'm drawn to the conclusion: guineas are smarter than they look.

Gazella is not just filled with vanity and mean-spiritedness; she is also known to show kindness on occasion. The years have mellowed her some. Our second group of young keets has a powder-blue colored female in its number. We call her Little Blue and Gazella likes her. She's chosen Little Blue to be her understudy in the art of gazing. They can be seen walking around the yard, chattering and gazing at themselves in anything shiny they can find; a puddle, a window, wheel rim, or bumper. They are equal opportunity gazers. Of course, Gazella's truck is always a popular option, but they are not exclusive. We purchased a used horse trailer and we have a step stool staged near it as we do necessary body work, repaint and restore it inside and out. As I've mentioned, guineas are incredibly curious creatures so they watch all our work with interest, passing often to survey our progress with the trailer.

We replaced the battered hubcaps on the trailer with shiny new ones. This has met with a flurry of appreciation from the girls. They jump up onto the step stool gaining them a perfect height to stare at themselves in the reflections made by the mirror-like finish of the chrome. They can be found there together nearly any time from morning to night, side by side on their own personal stage. I allow the guinea girls to use the step stool for a month, and then I put it away. The vantage point isn't as exciting to them without it, so they return to the truck with considerably less intensity than they displayed with the hubcaps and step stool.

Little Blue, though studying vanity with the pro, is not nearly as stuck on herself as Gazella. She desires motherhood. As the guineas travel around our property eating bugs and weed seeds, they hide their eggs in secluded places. They refuse to lay them in the nesting boxes I've provided; they want to collect them undisturbed in private. Little Blue takes note of these locations. She's gone missing to set on a clutch of eggs in a community nest. (Guineas and chickens lay eggs communally in a come one come all fashion of camaraderie.) She emerges briefly every day or two for a hurried drink and some feed from the hanging feeder in the coop, before returning for duty on her hidden nest. Little Blue never stays away from her eggs more than a few minutes; if eggs cool they will not hatch.

I watch the other guineas' behavior to try to learn where the nest is located. But, I'm unsuccessful in finding her. I can tell that Papa Guinea is spending time with her near the nest to keep guard over her because he is missing from his normal place within the group's daily rounds. He hurries to the coop at dusk, as the very last rays of shadow fall, in order to squeeze in before I close the door for the night. He is obviously torn between staying with her and the protection and routine of being with the flock. Nearly three weeks have gone on in this manner. The time is nearing the normal twenty-six to twenty-eight days needed to incubate guinea eggs.

Then one day I go out in customary fashion to release the birds for the day. Little Blue is waiting outside the closed door to the coop, plaintively calling to the other guineas. She's rumpled and harried looking. Her feathers are tattered and she is distraught. The other six guineas hurry down the ramp to encircle her within a ring they make of their bodies. They put their heads together in pow-wow fashion and "talk" to her gently. Next, they form two lines, one facing her head, the other facing her tail. Each group of three walks in these opposite directions, rubbing against her body, humming to her gently in order to console her. They continue this inexplicable behavior for seemingly interminable minutes. When they stop humming, she seems calmer. The comforters lead her to the coop for a long drink of water and a nourishing meal of feed. This is followed by more quiet humming and consoling.

An hour later, I glance out to see Little Blue with her companions filing out into the pasture; they walk behind her, single-file in solemn respect for her heartache. I hurry outside to follow them. I want to determine what has happened to her during the night. The solemn group moves slowly along, talking together. The birds stop when they reach a trail the horses have made while moving through a wooded section of our pasture. Once there, their vocal sounds rise from quiet humming to agitated screeching. Scattered on the ground below their feet lay little blue feathers. The group of mourners again circles Little

Blue to discuss the happenings of the night before. After a few moments, they open the circle of their bodies to let her pass. The concentration of feathers leads to an opening below a brush pile. Little Blue steps out of the circle to enter the brush pile's opening, scattered on its floor are broken egg shells, along with a few undamaged eggs. Some predator has raided her nest and she has barely escaped with her life.

Two or three nights pass while Little Blue grieves the loss of her cherished eggs. She and Papa stay out all night together, presumably at the nest site, grieving over the lost eggs and trying in vain to save the last unbroken ones remaining in the nest. When they are fully convinced that all hope is lost, they rejoin the flock.

It is very moving to see the compassion and gentleness the flock is displaying to her as she experiences her traumatic event. I am touched to see the depth of their concern for Little Blue. What insight God has instilled in them to help her in her time of need!

CHAPTER 10

DON'T GRIEVE TOO LONG

CHAPTER 10

DON'T GRIEVE TOO LONG

Our birds have free range of our acreage. They are generally content to stay within our pasture and mowed yard areas. The guineas range out much further on our property than the chickens do, sometimes they even venture out beyond our land. When the guineas start to stray, all we need to do is call a hearty, "Birdeeeees" and they will come running back from their errant journey. The shaking of the bird seed container in conjunction with the call tends to put a spring in their step.

In warm months, the foragers are mesmerized by the asphalt highway beyond our driveway, perhaps due to the insects that gather on the warm pavement. Regardless of the reason for their interest, their fascination with the road has made it the fiercest guinea predator we have had to fight.

One morning at 7:30, during the time our second group of young guineas were still "in training," I received a phone call informing me they were in the road. We live half a mile from the local school and it was time for school traffic to be at its peak. I hurried out to the road to discover traffic stopped from both directions. Two buses and several cars were halted from one side and a pair of cars from the other. Two of my adolescents had been hit and killed by a bus, another wounded and dazed; the remaining birds were running in circles around them screaming in alarm around their fallen friends. I shooed them all out of the road, allowing traffic to pass. I returned to the road, after giving my frantic guineas some wild bird seed to comfort them and distract them from following me back down the driveway.

Carefully gathering the wounded bird, I placed her beside the driveway to wait for me to complete my task. She was so dazed; she remained motionless in my absence. I placed a dead guinea on either side at the end of our driveway so the other guineas would see them there and remember the danger the road represented. It is a natural occurrence I had previously observed with them that whenever a predator attacks or kills one of their flock, they remember the area with suspicion and fear. They will approach the dangerous spot with caution or avoid the "death area" entirely. I was employing this concept in an attempt to keep them from the road.

After staging the dead birds by the driveway, I picked up the dazed bird. She was still so stunned as to rest her head on my shoulder while I carried her. Sadly I discovered the injured bird was Little Blue, Gazella's special friend. I feared she was badly injured because my guineas do NOT allow me to touch them. Guineas are much less domesticated than chickens and don't like cuddling, much to my chagrin. If she was cuddling, it looked serious indeed. I placed her gently in the rabbit hutch with food and water, praying for the best.

After finishing the bird seed, the confused survivors meander back down the driveway, chattering as they walk. Guineas are VERY vocal birds; they mutter, squawk, hum, chatter and scream in alarm about EVERYTHING. If you haven't had the pleasure of their company, it is impossible to imagine the range of sounds they are capable of. I only wish I could describe them to you adequately. Once the stunned survivors reach the scene of the accident, they stand in the driveway, next to the fallen bodies, craning their necks, circling them, screaming and yelling. The din settles to a dull roar as they mill about discussing the events that have occurred. The frightened birds stay close to the chicken coop for a few days in order to feel safer. They do stay out of the road for a few weeks after this, in response to the signposts of danger the dead birds represented. Although the bodies have been removed by some scavenging predator, no longer a visible reminder of the trauma, the memory of the event seemed to stay with them longer.

A few days of isolation and rest have revived Little Blue. She has started acting restless and calling to the others from her hutch, I've determined she is well enough to return to her companions. The other guineas are waiting outside the barn door in response to her calls and welcome her back warmly. Later in the day, my husband and I go out to check on her. We approach the whole guinea flock, but as we get closer to her specifically, the rest of the group circles around her as if in protection from our interest. One or two of them even run at us with wings arched in warning. She is theirs to care for, "Butt out," they seem to say.

Spring wears on into summer and Little Blue once again has become interested in motherhood. She is missing from the flock once more, reappearing every day or two to get a hurried drink and some laying crumbles. She is nesting in our front pasture, under a well-hidden clump of tall grass. After several attempts I finally locate her by following the movements of the other guineas.

Gazella also disappears from the ranks for parts of the day in order to keep Blue company. For the other parts of the day she returns to her only dependable friend, the Ford truck. Even if all her friends desert her, she can rely on her quiet, faithful companion to always be here for her. Little Blue carefully continues her nest setting duties until the longed for hatch day arrives. When I go out to let the rest of the flock free range for the day, Blue is proudly waiting at the foot of the chicken door exit ramp with six beautiful, bouncing babies. She's done it! This is the first successful guinea hatch we have witnessed performed by one of our guinea hens.

Previously I have tried incubator hatches and confining guinea hens in the rabbit hutch to protect them while setting for the nearly one month incubation period, which only resulted in a distraught bird nearly scrambling her eggs to escape confinement. The last method was one botched attempt in the front flower bed with Buffy standing guard over the bird at night. In Buffy's case it was the fox guarding the hen house. The eggs were close to hatching when she succumbed to the delectable temptation. This was discovered when we found Buffy barking at the guinea hen to get off the rest of her breakfast. Needless to say, all of these methods have met with limited success.

I am so pleased and Gazella is ecstatic! She races down the ramp, knocking the other birds out of her way like bowling pins as she pushes through to see the new keets. Gazella and Blue conscientiously dote over the babies as they parade them all over our property teaching them all they need to know for survival in the harsh world. My husband and I are amazed as we watch their resilience and energy. They run behind their "mommas" at break-neck speed, our eyes have difficulty following their movements as they dart to and fro. Whenever the shadow of a hawk passes overhead, their ever watchful moms shield them from the hawk's view by standing over them, effectively hiding them. The little family unit never pauses for a moment as this tactic is important to keep predators at bay. After the keets hatched, Little Blue is also avoiding the nest site for safety's sake. There are two unhatched eggs in the nest, undoubtedly rotten; that she knows will put off an odor to draw unwelcome attention. She keeps the kids far from this danger. Little Blue seems to feel her hatchlings are safer outside than they would be in the house with the rest of the birds, so she continues to hunker down somewhere with them each night.

My husband and I discuss capturing Little Blue and her babies to place them in the safety of the rabbit hutch in the barn. We know this would prove extremely challenging for us and perhaps even dangerous for the keets. Catching the keets in the fish net would be ineffective because the holes in the net are too large to capture the tiny bodies. Any other method we can dream up could crush them. The last thing we want to do is harm them after Little Blue's stellar hatching job! We decide not to meddle, just allowing her to continue the good work she is already doing so capably. One week after the hatch, it's Sunday morning and we are preparing ourselves for church and the ministry duties involved. We go out with joy and anticipation to see the progress of the growing keets. Little Blue is standing outside the coop as she had been the previous days, with the exception that there are now only two tiny babies huddling close to her legs instead of six. We are heart broken. Poor dear Blue, bereft of most of her brood. She has done everything so carefully, and yet they're still gone.

Life is so cruel. In mere moments our formerly eager and expectant hearts are now heavy and feel in need of some comfort, less prepared to minister to the needs of others. We have found our most disappointing events and heartrending bird-loss happens on Sundays. Emotional disappointments are most often thrown at us on the specific day when we are determined to serve God through our church's ministries to others. This causes us to conclude: discouragement comes on Sunday.

Gazella and Little Blue continue to gently mother the remaining keets, bravely carrying on despite the tragedy. Each day I eagerly go out in the morning expectant to see them. Today is Sunday. I go out to the coop — no Blue, no babies. A predator has killed them without a trace. Gazella is acting lost, unsure of what to do with her time. She dawdles near the chicken house waiting for them to appear. I'm sad for her. I'm sad for all of us. Yes indeed… discouragement comes on Sunday.

We have had a large number of birds come and go; dozens by now. We haven't stopped to count them. To the casual observer it might appear that we have become jaded about the deaths of our birds when they occur. That would not be an accurate assessment. Each little character holds a special place for us. Despite whether they lived long enough to be named or photographed, each one is a unique treasure. We are thankful for each moment we have had the privilege of sharing with them.

There are times when my husband and I wonder about our sanity as we continue to blunder our way through the whole silly process of bird ownership. Why bother? one might ask. In answer to the question we recall all the moments of entertainment they provide us, as well as the tick-free strolls in our yard and we conclude we would do it all over again anyway. We are choosing to focus on the joy of their lives, not the sorrow of their deaths. We're learning we shouldn't grieve too long or we'll miss the joy that's coming next.

CHAPTER 11

SAVOR THE MOMENT

CHAPTER 11

SAVOR THE MOMENT

Immediately after we lost Blue and her babies we purchase new guinea hatchlings. Our numbers of adults have dwindled again. We need more tick eaters on duty. We also want some babies to comfort my husband and me as well as poor bereaved Gazella.

We wonder how she'll respond to the keets, but she seems so pleased to greet them. Once she hears their little peeps, she comes running to see them and hangs around close to the rabbit hutch in the barn as if watching them grow. As soon as they are old enough for her to take over raising them, she jumps in with the intensity we have come to expect of her in anything she does. Gazella is finally mothering!

It took her four years to embrace the idea, but she is terrific at it. Under her tutelage, none of the guineas venture into the road. She's taught them how to navigate the coop's entry ramp and to identify our vehicles so they can come begging for bird seed snacks. She runs a tight ship. No one steps out of line or she charges at them, wings spread and beak lashing at the offender. Gazella is a firm, but fair disciplinarian. The keets know what the rules are as well as what the penalty will be for breaking them.

"Momma is only telling you once," she seems to say. There is no sassing or backtalk allowed.

We now have a lovely male guinea with a white speckled breast that the books describe as pied color. We call him The Pied Peeper. He is one of the new leaders among our group. He is extremely intrigued by human activities. The Peeper and his entourage spend long hours watching us through our windows. They stand on windowsills and front porch furniture for the best view into our home and its goings on. As we sit quietly on the couch, we hear the calls of The Peeper and his buddies. At times, only one head is visible above the sill of the window, but on closer inspection, we see all the guineas and some of the chickens napping on the bench or on the table of our porch.

The bird seed snacks are a strong draw, but I'm convinced the snacks are not the only reason my birds seek out my company. I believe that they truly like me. They want to be involved in everything I do, both inside and outside of our house. They make this very obvious in their hurried steps to join me as I engage in any work or fun outside. Before my husband and I saddle up our horses, the guineas walk to the pasture with us to halter them and stand nearby to watch us put on their saddles; commenting from the sidelines. They follow along behind us as we ride partway down the driveway, going as far as Buffy's electric fence boundary line. There they stop following us and join Buffy in her vocal complaints at being left behind as we ride away. They make a ridiculous picture standing and shouting together. The Pit Bull and her posse.

I purchased a tiny rooster, although the chicken breeder sold him to me assuming he was a hen. We named him Jumping Jack Flash. He is much smaller than the Silkie roosters, New Furbee or Benny. Weighing in at close to one pound, with skinny, long legs and a riot of flashy colors to his feathers, Jack Flash's personality matches his flashy appearance. He is a study in perpetual motion and near constant crowing. Over the telephone my dad says his high pitched crow reminds him of a rusty gate hinge. He is a darling rooster! He isn't combative, just proud. He doesn't fight with my other three roosters. No advances toward any people either. He's all I believe a bantie should be. He's entertaining to me and good to the hens.

Our youngest son visited with us and brought his half-grown miniature Daschund, Prince Charming, into our menagerie. Prince has never seen chickens or guineas, and he finds them irresistible. He runs at the flock, scattering them in alarm. The guineas gather in a group to block him from the other birds and yell at him. They are aware he's a strange dog, not family. Prince however, showed little concern for the scolding he received, running enthusiastically behind Jumping Jack Flash. Jumping Jack however, is concerned by Prince! Living up to his name, Jumping Jack jumps up and flies across the yard to roost in a tree twenty feet above ground, well out of reach of his pursuer. Jumping Jack is also yelling at Prince. I assume it means something like, "NaNaNa Boo Boo, you can't get me;" but I can't be sure. I have never seen a chicken fly, though I've seen them flutter and jump while flapping their wings. Jumping Jack was evidently 'highly' motivated!!

Jack Flash's beautiful little mate is a delicate black and white hen, tiny like him, with frizzle, an unusual feather structure. The frizzle gene causes feathers to stand up on end with a kinked look as though they were put in a crimping iron. Her name is Miss Frizz. She and Jumping Jack Flash are the perfect couple. I don't see one without the other… it must be love.

Miss Frizz has laid some incredibly tiny eggs in the chicken house. Polly took notice and is soon setting on them. After several days, Frizzie wants in on the setting action. She joins Polly and they set in the box, side by side or back to back, whichever suits their mood at any given time. Frizzie takes more breaks than Polly does, but working together, the eggs are always covered. Frizzie's eggs were not the only ones beneath the girls. Polly and Frizzie had been collecting all the hen's eggs over an extended period of time. I didn't know which eggs had been deposited when. This made determining the exact hatch date problematic. I watched and waited expectantly. The day arrived; how exciting.

It's Jumping Jack and Miss Frizzie's babies! Talk about cute! They are the tiniest hatchlings I have ever seen. The hens begin caring for them right in the chicken coop with the grownups. Aside from a small food and water container on the floor at their reach and some newspapers to keep their little feet from falling through the wire, I don't have to adjust things for them. This is the first time the weather has been cooperative for the chicks to grow up with their moms. This should be much simpler.

There are still several eggs under them, unhatched, so I'm still waiting. I think I'll give it a couple more days, and then remove them. I looked in on the babies this morning and to my horror, find a revolting odor and two gooey and unhappy chicks. I should have removed those eggs yesterday; we had a bad egg explosion overnight. Poor Polly and the babies got gooed! Fortunately for Miss Frizz, she was on break when the accident happened. Wow, what a stink! You can bet I'm moving quickly to remove the last ones before any more mishaps occur!

The chicks dried off and the goo went away, I'm not sure where. Oh well, some questions are not really meant to be answered. In spite of the goo event, the teeny babies are thriving with the big kids. They are really hearty. I'm so glad this is going so well.

I just returned from a Wednesday evening prayer meeting at church, my husband is working a night shift, so he's not with me. I went out to lock up my birds since it was still light out and they were still outside playing and refused go to bed before I left. When I look inside the door, I see feathers everywhere. Back in a corner, by the nesting boxes sits an opossum crouched over the lifeless body of little Miss Frizz. One tiny chick has been trampled to death in the melee and the other is screaming in fear back in a corner. I can't find Polly, Jumping Jack Flash, The Pied Peeper or Ginger. I can generally keep a cool head in such instances, but this doesn't seem to be a cool-headed moment. I run in the house to find a weapon, with the intention of killing the intruder. I have had the unfortunate experience of varmint disposal before this occasion, but it isn't something I am adept at, nor do I want to do it. I much prefer a "live and let live" approach; but he had crossed the line when he ate Miss Frizz! So I run to the house intending to get a weapon; blubbering inconsolably as I ran. *Not Miss Frizz! Not the Babies!! No!!!*

After examining the weapons choices, I decide that my birds have met with enough tragedy tonight without me causing more mayhem by blasting about wildly with a weapon in my distraught state. I call a friend to come help me. She and her husband bring a handgun and shoot the predator.

My friends and I search for the other birds. We find Polly outside in the dark, crying for the babies. We put her back with the last remaining chick, hoping for a miracle to save it from the chill and shock it has received. Oh good, there's Jumping Jack! He's so disoriented that he lets me pick him up without even running away. He appears uninjured. Where is Ginger? No sign of her. No Peeper either.

How strange again, that such an emotionally devastating event happened again on a church day; after spending time learning about God through studying the Bible, as well as being encouraged by spending time with our church family. I feel that it is a spiritual attack, sent to discourage me in my Christian walk. I'm once again stricken with the notion, discouragement can come any day, and it isn't limited to Sunday.

In the morning I let the birds out, Peeper is by the ramp waiting for the others to exit the coop. He is hurt. One wing is badly damaged. I try to catch him with the fish net before letting the others out, which would only add to the chaos of my attempts to net him. Unfortunately, he won't let me catch him. Once they exit the coop, he joins the other guineas for the day. He doesn't seem to be moving too badly. Still no sign of Ginger. I have a feeling she's fallen prey to some other predator as she ran frightened into the dark. The tiny baby perished. Polly's body warmth could not undue the trauma to his fragile system. So much for this chicken hatch being simple. Life is never simple.

Night comes again. I go out a little early before full dark to put some bird seed out to coax the birds safely inside. I call and call for the guineas. They answer me and come close, but refuse to come inside the coop. They won't leave Peeper alone and he's too frightened to enter the dangerous place where his injury occurred. I can't convince him that the chicken coop is safe now, since he knows it wasn't safe last night. I still can't catch him with the net. The other guineas fly up into their favorite cedar tree to roost for the night, but Peeper's wing is too wounded for flight. He hides in the tall grass. There's nothing I can do to protect him.

It's morning again. Praise God, Peeper made it through the night. The others are nurturing him with tender care. I think he'll mend if I can just get him back into the house tonight. I'm pondering methods of capture, but I'm afraid I'll injure him even more severely if I try any other methods. I feel so helpless.

It's morning again. No Peeper. The other guineas are safe, but I find a cluster of his feathers in the tall grass. I heave a sigh and fall back into discouragement again. I decide to intentionally take a moment to remember the laughter that came from observing the antics of all my little lost friends. Those that were lost today as well as those gone before them. Ginger; the New Hampshire Red hen who followed me everywhere. As fast as she could stretch her legs she came running, in a silly pull up the pantaloons gesture that always made me laugh out loud. She was the first to greet me wherever I was in the yard. Once when unloading groceries from the hatchback of my car, I returned from taking a load into the house to find her IN my car, investigating my purchases. She even asked to be held on occasion. I'm glad to have known her.

Each of my birds has added depth and substance to my life. Peeper; gawking into the house to ask, "Whatcha Doin'?" in his own distinct questioning tone. I will never forget my sweet Pearl. She was a priceless tribute to friendship and motherhood. Papa is still a fresh memory as I recall him parading the new keets past my blackberry patch as I worked in the garden. He hadn't noticed my presence until the moment he was intending to teach the keets how to steal berries. He came to an abrupt halt, nonchalantly changing direction, all but whistling, pretending they were out for an innocent stroll. I never could have conceived that birds are capable of such creative thought and pretense. Who would have thought?

There was a time when I was working in the garage near dusk and heard the guineas throwing a shrieking fit behind our house. They carried on for ten or fifteen minutes, their tones escalating in intensity so I knew they thought there was real danger. I recognized their vocal tones as the danger alarm. When I went to investigate, I saw that a coyote was approaching the chicken coop. I found our then seven guineas in V-formation standing off the coyote in order to protect the chickens. They were holding the line to prevent his advance. When I arrived, the coyote fled. I believe it was about to be frightened away by the guinea patrol and I just hastened the process. I've also seen them chase off strange dogs from the yard and pasture.

I have learned many things while watching my birds; one of which is that life can be very short. That concept doesn't seem to bother my feathered friends. No ominous shadow hangs over their heads. They enjoy each moment without a care in the world. It's delightful to observe their daily activities and peaceful manner. Sometimes I worry for them, since they don't know how. Other times I remember that life is fleeting for all of us, human and fowl alike. None of us knows how many days we will be blessed with. We should live each one to the fullest in a manner that would please God our creator. It's interesting to reflect on the many ways that one life affects another… even the life of a mere bird.

Even as I savor the moments, I'm surprised to think of how many details of my fowl life have already faded. The events I thought I could never forget are already beginning to grow hazy in my memory. Many of the little individuals whose antics have entertained me have already lived a short yet meaningful life. The enjoyment I received from observing them will live on in my heart in an immeasurable way. I'm inspired by their example as I go about my daily life, I have an opportunity to lift up and encourage those around me, in small or large ways.

However, this sad experience is not the end of the tale. I now have an incubator filled with twenty four Belgium D'Uccle eggs and two Leghorn eggs. Perhaps I will find another gentle hen like my sweet Pearl?

CHAPTER 12

TODAY IS HATCH DAY

CHAPTER 12

TODAY IS HATCH DAY!

Today is hatch day and I can hardly wait to see what joy awaits. When I woke up I hurried downstairs to the incubator to see what's happening. The eggs are starting to pip, which means the chicks are starting to poke tiny holes in the eggshell with their beaks to crack them. The eggs are rolling gently as the chicks stretch their bodies in an effort to break free from the shell walls that confine them. I can hear them peeping softly from beneath the protective layer of their egg shell and see them peck their beaks against it, nibbling at the tiny hole which they've already poked. I watch with wonder as I realize the power it takes for the cramped chicks to break out of those very hard shells. They have been rolled into a compact ball within the shell as they form, but God equips them with all the tools they need to break free and start life in the big world outside.

The process of hatching is taking several hours as the chicks work, wiggle, peck, squirm and then rest awhile before continuing. Once it wiggles free of its shell, wet and tired, one of the chicks lays on the floor of the incubator to rest from the hard work of hatching. Another totters around unsteadily, stretching its legs. Their legs have been curled up for three long weeks during development in their shell. It will take them several hours to stiffen up and straighten out as they dry. I'll leave them alone to finish drying and check later to see how many more will hatch as the day goes on.

By suppertime when I check again, I find that something has gone wrong with the hatch. There is only one more hatched chick. Hatch day is already one day later than it should have been; twenty-two days instead of twenty-one. Out of the twenty-six eggs, only the three have hatched. I place the last hatched chick in the rabbit hutch with the others to warm under the lamp.

In the morning I proceed to candle the remaining eggs to determine what is happening in there. Candling is done using a bright light and a dark room. I take the eggs out of the incubator one by one, moving quickly so they don't get chilled, just in case there are any more healthy chicks ready to hatch. I take an egg and hold it cupped in my hand while shining the flashlight up through the egg so I can see if the egg is fertile, partly or fully developed; or even whether the chick is alive. The determination is made according to what I see through the eggshell. I find eight eggs are infertile and the remaining chicks have developed. I know this because the eggshells are full, which means no light can pass through them. There is no apparent movement inside the eggs. I can't hear the chicks move when I place the eggs near my ear and the eggs aren't moving on the incubator floor as they would during active hatching. This information indicates the chicks died late in the development phase. This could be due to incubator temperature or humidity variations within the incubator. I decide to wait another day to allow for the possibility of any stragglers that I'm mistaken about. I'll remove the eggs after that.

Meanwhile of course, there are live babies to care for. When I check the chicks in the rabbit hutch I see our tiny late hatch baby sitting on its round bottom, legs sprawled out straight to the side. It looks very much like ice-skating gone awry. The little legs have gone ZING! – whizzing out in either direction, giving no support at all. The poor little fella can't stand or walk. This is very serious indeed. It also means he can't get to food or water.

I pick up the chick to assess his tiny legs for abnormalities in leg function, bending each individual joint to see if it moves properly. At first each joint is stiff and slow to bend, but as I very gently work each one, they loosen up. It doesn't appear that anything is malformed, but his hips just refuse to stay close to his sides in support of his weight. Hmmm... *now what?*

I hurry into the house to call the chicken breeder from whom I purchased the eggs. I tell her about the hatching challenges I'm encountering and ask her input about what may have gone wrong so I can correct it for next time. When she finds out how many infertile eggs there were, she offers to replace the eggs for free; saying that she is very disappointed in her roosters for not doing their job. I gratefully accept her gracious offer, thankful for another chance at a good sized hatch.

We then discuss the invalid chick. I describe his infirmity and she explains that this is called "spraddle leg". Thankfully there is a treatment for it. I'm so relieved since helpless creatures tug at my heartstrings. It would have been so hard to stand by unable to help it.

Ironically, the chicken-breeder is also a nurse, so she explained the procedure to me in perfect nurse-speak. She also told me of a chicken care website that provides videos for a visual of how to do the work. I don my nurse's cap and watch a quick video to be sure I understand the concept. Then after gathering materials; one adult size Band-Aid cut in half lengthwise, (better bring a couple in case I'm not proficient), scissors, and my husband as a helper to hold the little chick while I do the nursing work; we set out for the barn.

The information I gathered explained the process as follows:

1. Cut one adult size Band-Aid in half lengthwise.
2. Remove cover from adhesive on one end of Band-Aid.
3. Attach adhesive to base of chicken leg, near the hock-joint.
4. Use nonstick pad as center spacer between legs.
5. Remove other cover from adhesive on other end of Band-Aid.
6. Attach adhesive to base of other chicken leg, near hock-joint.
   (Can you see why I need the video? Sounds like Greek to me.)

My husband and I are discussing the medical particulars as we walk. (Have I mentioned that I tend to make a production out of things?) When we arrive at the barn I reach in to grab out our teeny patient, again vocalizing my expectations of my helper. Using an encouraging, "we can do this" cheerleader style, I rattle on in a non-stop, rapid-fire monologue. "The idea here is leg splints. We have to support his legs under him so he can stand. His hips aren't staying together, so somehow we've got to manipulate those hips to get under him and stay there. Is this making sense to you?" I ask, not pausing long enough to allow a response. "I'm not sure I quite understand yet. Well, maybe it will make sense once I get started. The video said he should be right as rain by morning; or at most in a couple of days. I'm going to tape the left leg first. Oops, the tape stuck to his foot. Sorry, I need another Band-Aid. Hold his legs closer please." My husband patiently holds the little chick, legs pointed up to give me access to them.

The chick is calm and surprisingly silent while we work, seeming to trust us. Most times if you remove a chick from its pen it cheeps loudly in protest at being held. This chick seems strangely comforted by our handling.

My lack of proficiency is becoming evident and tensions are mounting between medical personnel. We agree that future splinting sessions will be done without my patient helper being present. "I think I can do it by myself next time." I say. "Great!" says he.

After MUCH hoopla… the newly splinted baby is placed gently on his feet. He does a rapid nose-dive followed by a roll onto his side. There he lies, paddling in the air, helpless. This was not the outcome I expected. "Maybe his little legs will get stronger from the exercise of kicking like that, and his legs do need to get used to not being spraddled out at his sides," I muse. We both walk away trying not to watch his futile struggles, hoping our efforts have given him a chance at a healthy life.

My husband and I went about our day. It was a Saturday and my husband was home all day with me. We had a lot of spring yard work to do, so we each conquered a different project. When we paused for a short break my husband said, "I gave the baby a drink and put some chick feed by him so he could reach it." In unspoken agreement from then on, we took turns stopping by to check on the chick. Pausing frequently as we passed the barn to dip his beak in the water, as well as making sure he had food to sustain him until he could manage on his own.

I remembered a Bible reference in II Samuel 4:4 that referred to King Saul's grandson being lame in his legs, his name was Mephibosheth. The Bible verse reads as follows: And Jonathan, Saul's son had a son that was lame of his feet… and his name was Mephibosheth. I donned our tiny baby with the very big name. I think it fits him just right. Mephibosheth became my instant favorite, I can't help myself. I guess I'm a sucker for the underdog. It should be noted here that Mephibosheth is a porcelain-colored D'Uccle just like my dear, departed Pearl was. That might sway things in his favor as well.

We continued this scenario for two days until I found 'my baby' had rolled away from the heat lamp, away from the covered area I had carefully prepared for the chicks to protect them from the wire floor. His tiny wing nub was wedged in the wire squares of the hutch's floor. Poor dear 'Phibby' was cold, cheeping pitifully and breathing in a shallow, stressed out way. I gave him a drink and put him under the heat-lamp with chick starter by his face hoping he would eat.

Back to the internet for more research. How long does it take for a spraddle-leg chick to recover? I query. Some say a day or two. Some say a week. I finally stumble onto a helpful site that mentions placing the chick inside a three-inch diameter plastic pot that plants come in. The idea here is the chick's body is supported in an upright position by the padded sides of the pot. The chick cannot fall onto its side; therefore, its legs grow stronger as they're exercised by its own movements within the pot. For instance, he can squat down to sleep or stand up on tippy-toes to try to see what the other chicks are doing. This flower-pot-exercise-contraption reminds me of a device we had for our oldest son. It hung from a doorway with the child's feet slipped through openings in a harness, feet dangling, barely touching the floor. Through bouncing action the child could "jump up" and down to strengthen their legs for the purpose of walking. (These contraptions were all the rage in the early 1980s.) Since I had personally witnessed the effectiveness of the Johnny-Jump-Up, I was certain this idea would also work.

I surveyed my collection of plastic containers for a suitable one for the job. Since Phibby is a bantie and therefore short of stature, I decide on a blueberry box. I think the height of the flower pot might be too deep. I don't want him to smother in there. I pad the inside of the box, cushioning the floor as well so his feet won't slip. My chicken exerciser will not use the "dangling feet" effect. My chick's feet will be supported by the floor of his device.

I effectively create a "Johnny-Jump-Up" exerciser to support Phibby in an upright position until his legs get stronger. I enact this plan and place him inside the contraption expectantly. I then place the exerciser and chick close enough to the heat-lamp to maintain his body temperature without overheating him. I walk away to let him settle in.

When I return five minutes later to check on him, I am surprised to find that his legs are stronger than I had previously estimated. He has ejected himself out of his blueberry box and he's now lying on his side paddling frantically in the air again. This gives me hope about his long term prognosis; he's getting stronger. I go back inside the house to get the three-inch flower pot, swapping the padding from the blueberry box, I reposition Phibby again. After several checks to tweak the position of his pot and its proximity to the heat-lamp, I go to bed.

When I hurry out to the barn in the morning to check Phibby, my heart jumps in alarm. He's huddled down within his pot, very still. Did he overheat in there? Or smother, or get too cold? I pick him up to find, silly me, he's just sleeping! What a relief. I dip his beak for a quick drink before the moment of truth; has there been any change in his condition over night?

With great hope, I set Phibby gently on his feet, ready to catch him if he nose-dives. I watch in joy as he stands! He totters slightly, taking tiny hopping steps, his feet are anchored together after all, teetering toe to heel as he finds his balance. All the physical therapy has paid off. With the support of his Band-Aid leg braces, his feet can't spraddle, all the joints and muscles must learn their new jobs, but I can see that it is going to work. Whew, what a relief! Twelve hours of Johnny-Jump-Up therapy have done the job. I don't think Phibby needs the contraption any longer; it has quickly and effectively done its job.

I decide Phibby will be better off out moving around with his fellow hatchlings than he would be in his exerciser. I leave him free, monitoring his progress often. By afternoon Phibby is already remarkably improved. He's hopping around with the other kids, from food to water, lying down to nap and rising to stand once he wakes. He is now capable of eating and drinking by himself and he starts to gain weight and size. The growth is nearly visible from moment to moment. He looks less like the underdog each time I check on him. It's official… he's going to make it.

Our pastor and his family came over today. Their five children were anxious to see the new babies. When at church the previous evening, I had explained all the concerns and procedures of caring for Phibby. Pastor's oldest daughter who is nine had been present, listening with rapt attention as I told dear Phibby's tale. The children disembarked from their van, amid much enthusiasm, all talking at once about what they wanted to see first. "Can we gather eggs?" "I want to see the horses." "Where are the guineas at?" The oldest girl immediately asked me, "Can I see "The Potted Chick"?" What a clever title; she has obviously thought a lot about this! We all agreed together that seeing all the new chicks was a good starting point for their visit to the farm.

We all went out to the barn to witness the "Potted Chick's" miracle recovery. The kids took turns holding the chicks. It is evident that Phibby enjoys being held. He doesn't squirm, cheep or try to hide his face like the others do. I wonder if it's just from the extra handling he has received as I doctor him. I don't believe that I would feel endeared to someone who held me upside down and taped my legs together, but apparently Phibby doesn't resent it.

By the next day, I must replace Phibby's leg splints. In his exuberance for hopping, he's wiggled one adhesive side loose. Without the support however, he can't stand alone yet, so I put the splint back on. As I check on his progress throughout the day I see him taking steps, one foot first and then the other. He can't move his feet very far due to the restraint of his braces, but he's getting the hang of it.

On the following day he's pulled the braces loose again. He's standing well, but still a little spraddle-legged and in need of support for another few days I believe. I put his braces back on again. Hey, I discover I'm starting to get proficient at this. Apparently all it takes is a little practice.

After a few short days of wearing legs splints little Phibby is nearly caught up in size with the other kids. He's moving fine now, although every day I have to re-tape him till his legs get stronger. On day seven I decide to remove the splints and see how he does without them. He takes a tiny faltering step unused to the full reach of motion afforded him without the tape's restriction. The next step is longer than the last, each succeeding step lengthening until Phibby has found his perfect stride. He's off and running now! How heartwarming it is to see how far he's come.

I suspect there may be some reading this who will wonder why I bothered to save this one injured chick. That's a lot of time and effort for a chicken, you might be thinking. In response I would say my heart couldn't help but go out to the tiny, helpless baby. The idea of just letting him die was not an option I could bear to consider. As I looked at him and realized his need for help, the healthy birds faded to the background. Though I gave the strong chicks all the care they needed, I doted on Phibby. The wounded individual was my necessary focus.

I'm so thankful God also cares about the individual. He displays that same loving concern for my life on a daily basis, in the big things as well as the small ones. I often find myself saying aloud, "Thank you Lord. I don't understand why you even care about this. I'm so glad you notice me."

I see God's hand in all the things around me, through nature and animals of course, but most especially in the details of my life. As I go to God in prayer, I'm confident in the knowledge that God will answer me when I ask for his help. I know this because he has answered my prayers, very specifically and repeatedly. I can come to him about anything. Nothing is too small or big for God to be interested in.

I've seen his concern for me in the small things like finding little Pearl that dark night when I asked for his help, finding a misplaced item (many times–*sigh*), intervening in specific health needs, financial and emotional cares and the safety of family or other loved ones as well as numerous other specific answers to my requests. I find it amazing the God of the universe cares about these insignificant things in one individual's life.

Phibby has given me the joy I hoped would come with the incubator hatch. Not only in the feeling of accomplishment I received from saving his life, but in the entertainment he provided through his endearing capers. My husband and I have watched him behave in ways we've never seen any of our other birds do. He kicks his little feathered feet in an angry bull gesture when we hold one of his buddies. We don't know if he wants to be held in their place or whether he misses their company with him, but his displeasure is evident. His most common maneuver involves pointing his nose down, nearly touching the floor of his pen. His wings spread out at an angle, much like you see in the old movies where the pilot and co-pilot are going through the take-off sequence before flight.

Propeller, check.

Flaps, check.

Landing gear, check.

All the while scooting his feet backwards in rapid foot-fires. It looks like he's trying to gain steam for flight. During these maneuvers he'll often pop up in the air to grab a wayward insect as it flies by. We've speculated this may be a birdie dominance ritual. We are mesmerized as we watch him perform it. It's like watching a great online-video; we wish we could play it over and over.

A surprising revelation occurred one day when I noted that the other chicks had developed combs and Phibby had not. It became evident that "he" is a "she". Phibby has the potential to become a wonderful mother as was Pearl; she has been given a chance at a full life through the compassion shown to her.

The next load of incubator chicks have also hatched; thirteen out of eighteen! What fun they are to watch. Phibby is showing a propensity for mothering. When the tiny ones, which are one month younger than her, get scared, she shelters them under her wings. She enjoys being held by humans and has a delicate beauty that is growing day by day. Phibby was worth the effort it took to save her!

CHAPTER 13

TODDLERS AND HATCHLINGS

CHAPTER 13

TODDLERS AND HATCHLINGS

When I made the decision to purchase eggs instead of chicks, little did I know how that one choice would change the whole bird raising experience. There were several factors involved in the final decision. Because of selecting a large number of eggs to hatch, I was able to choose the exact birds I wanted to keep from a larger pool of choices. This enabled me to choose the color, temperament and sex of the bird. If I had answered an advertisement for chicks for sale I would have been at the mercy of availability; for instance, the seller might have said, "I have two porcelain roosters and one mille fleur hen, but if you'll wait a month or two, I might have more." I had a better chance to get just what I was after in my chosen time table by raising them myself.

Another factor was cost. Instead of paying five to ten dollars per bird for the four birds I wanted, I paid ten dollars for eighteen eggs. This enabled me to choose from the hatched chicks to select the ones I desired to keep and sell or give away the surplus. This method also offset the cost of electricity involved in running the incubator and heat lamp. It was not a get rich quick scheme by any stretch of the imagination, but it has been fun while accomplishing the desired goals.

I also wanted a new group of guineas to replenish the ever dwindling population we donate to the highway in front of our house. (Guineas can't eat ticks in our yard if they are safely confined to protect them from the road; therefore, we do lose some to the road. It's a sad hard fact of guinea life.) I had been watching ads to find guinea keets for purchase; however, I wasn't having any luck. I found seven of our guinea eggs conveniently deposited in the chicken coop just begging to be incubated. This was a rare and timely occurrence. I seldom find them in the coop; they are usually out in a field, hidden in the tall grass. I had just picked up the D'Uccle eggs from the chicken breeder, so I placed the guinea eggs in the incubator with them. How very serendipitous. I would only have to go through the long drawn out process of youngster raising once. Instead of having to incubate, then rabbit hutch brood with a light, acclimate to outdoor temperature, place in wire cage to integrate with adult birds in coop, open wire cage door within the coop, teach to navigate ramp, catch with fish net when they're too dopey to find their way into the coop at bedtime, etc., etc., in two groups. I could do it once and be finished. I'm sure I make the process sound REALLY simple, but it is complicated and lo-o-o-n-g, lasting a minimum of three months from start to finish. Even though I enjoy the process it starts to wear a little thin by the end. I was certain that once would be enough to satisfy my inner nurturer.

My carefully premeditated, seamless hatching plan, as with most plans did not go as expected. I had forgotten when I placed the two different types of eggs in the incubator together that they hatch at different times. Chickens hatch at twenty-one days and guineas at twenty-six to twenty-eight days. That doesn't sound problematic, but it is due to the egg-turner we use in the incubator. The egg-turner had already complicated things when its motor burned out early on in the process, causing me to have to manually turn eggs three times a day until a replacement turner came in the mail. It is important that the egg-turner be removed two days before scheduled hatch day to ensure that newly hatched chicks don't get caught and injured or crushed by the rotating trays that hold the eggs. So my problem was this: the chickens didn't need the egg-turner any longer, but the guineas did, and if I opened the incubator top to manually turn the guinea eggs, I would chill the chicks during their hatch. The guinea eggs wouldn't hatch well without being turned; it's a catch-22.

Time to find a solution. Aha! Pearl's daughter Polly wanted to hatch eggs. She would be thrilled. She'd been sitting day after day in an empty nesting box just dying for some real eggs to set on. I gathered up the guinea eggs, stuck them under Polly and waited. According to my calculations it should be another week before the keets will hatch under her.

Earlier than expected, just two days after the three previously mentioned D'Uccle chicks hatched, I found Polly outside her nesting-box, on the floor of the coop, crouched over two live guinea keets. There was also a third keet, lying dead in the water dispenser I had set out in advance for the babies when they arrived. (Guineas are NOT very bright! Though to be fair to their intellect, they crawl into the water to try to warm themselves. I've been told that they will only drown themselves if they are cold.) The tiny keets couldn't hop back up the three-inch lip of the nesting box front to return to Polly for warmth after they ate and drank, so she went to them instead. She did a great job of protecting the hatched keets, but that meant that the unhatched eggs cooled and now wouldn't hatch. Raising guineas is a very complicated undertaking. It's a good thing I enjoy a challenge!

I had fully intended to leave the guinea keets with Polly so she could raise and teach them, but now it was looking unwise. The keets had already demonstrated their inability to maneuver the nesting box sides when getting to food and water. The spring weather was still cool and the babies would need a heat lamp unless Polly continued to hover over them in the middle of the newspaper covered coop floor. I decided to move them out to the rabbit hutch with the three D'Uccle chicks who did have a heat lamp they could share.

The first step was to place pebbles in the water to prevent drownings. I then placed them in the hutch with the chicks. They took to it quite naturally, acting as though they were also chicks. My husband and I had been holding the D'Uccle chicks several times daily to encourage them to be docile. We implemented the same treatment plan for the keets. They didn't take to that "naturally". Whenever we reached our hands anywhere in remote proximity to them, they would squawk, scream and flee as quickly as they could in the opposite direction. I'm proud to say, we persevered in continuing our attempts to handle them. Despite the claims we've heard about guineas enjoying handling, we have certainly not had any experiences that support that claim. They staunchly resisted our attempts to tame them.

When the next chick hatch occurred from the replaced eggs, I placed the new chicks in with the three older chicks. The thirteen newly hatched D'Uccle chicks were blending seamlessly with the older chicks and keets. Birds are notoriously unwelcoming to newcomers, often chasing them from food and water or even pecking them to death. However, to my surprise, I had no squabbling in the group as I continued to add new birds.

Another fortuitous event happened right after the second incubator hatch finished. A neighbor whom I had not previously met pulled up in the driveway to say hello. He explained that he's noticed my guineas and is a fellow guinea owner. He raises guineas and several breeds of laying chickens. "If you ever need replacement guineas, I raise them. I have keets hatching now," he informed me. This was great news. I had hoped for four to six from the hatch with Polly, but with the complications that cropped up, had ended up with only two. I told him I would love to purchase a few keets from him. He graciously brushed away my attempts to pay for them, displaying a "this is what neighbors do for one another" generosity.

A few days later he called to say that he had two keets ready to go. He brought them over and I placed them in the rabbit hutch with the other young birds. All went well for two days, until I couldn't find the newest keets in the hutch with the sixteen D'Uccle chicks and two guinea keets that they were rooming with. (You may be thinking that it sounds a little crowded in their hutch, but all the hatchlings were very tiny. Space was not an issue. They had no need to escape.)

In my search for the lost keets, I looked beside the hutch to find one of the new keets upside down, feet stuck straight up in the air, wedged in a gap in our nearby firewood stack, cheeping pitifully. The keet was cold and one wing was stiff from being propped at an odd angle. I popped him back under the heat lamp and searched for the other keet; to no avail. Due to the impossibility of escape from the covered top of the hutch, I surmised that the new keets had squeezed themselves through the ½ inch wire squares that comprise the sides of the hutch. I would never have believed they could fit through such a tiny space, but I have observed their "Houdini" antics in older keets when squeezing through the wire under our chicken coop. Guinea keets are a bit like hamsters, if their head can fit through an opening, they can squeeze their body through too. I immediately proceeded to cut strips of cardboard to line the inside of the hutch, up about four inches to prevent additional bailout attempts.

A few days later my new friend and neighborhood guinea supplier brought three more recruits to add to my ragtag bunch. I placed them in the hutch with all the others, including the now recovered former escapee. That addition of keets brought me up to the six keets I had planned for. I sure took the long route of gathering them up, however. You know by now how much I enjoy a production. It seems that nothing I do is accomplished without one.

My husband and I continued to handle the youngsters, though I must admit, our enthusiasm for handling keets was low. We did it out of a sense of stubbornness, a sort of 'I'm going to hold you and you are going to like it' type attitude. The chicks on the other hand are pure joy to hold. They actually enjoy being held. A fact they make clear by flying and hopping up towards us when we open the hutch lid. Several special chicks walk towards our hands when we reach in to pick them up and come right back to us if we put them down to pick up a different chick in their place.

Little Phibby won a special place in my husband's heart and I often go outside to see him sitting on our wooden swing holding her in his lap. She likes the attention and is as soft as velvet. She continues to nurture the younger chicks and is strong and healthy with no visible evidence of her rough beginnings.

By this point our babies are separated into two rabbit hutches. One hutch is located in the barn to house guinea keets and roosters. I have moved the hens and the one rooster I intend to keep into the other hutch a few yards from our chicken coop. One hutch is no longer roomy enough for twenty-two young birds; they need room to stretch out.

The youngsters are now eight weeks and twelve weeks respectively and it's time to find homes for any D'Uccles that I'm not intending to keep. I place an ad for purebred Bantams and wait for the calls to flood in; I'm confident that everyone would want them if they only knew how special they are. As predicted, new families arrive and make their selections. They are indeed impressed with my delightful babies.

In the midst of the bird raising and re-homing activities, our granddaughters are coming to stay with us. Millie is four and Harper is one-and-a-half. Millie adores 'Grandma Laura's birds' and has been beside herself, knowing she will get to see and hold them. As I spoke with Millie on the phone prior to her arrival, she was literally screaming in anticipation. Look out birdies, here she comes!

I drove a couple hours to meet our daughter-in-law for the child exchange. The whole return trip is punctuated with joyful exclamations of, "I can't wait to hold baby birdies!" As soon as we get disentangled from our car seats and seat belts, respectively, Grandpa gets nary a sideways glance of greeting. We are off to see the baby birdies. Hugs will have to wait.

Millie squeals loudly, hands aflutter, trembling with exuberance, "They're SO CUTE!!! Can I hold that itsy bitsy tiny one?" She has selected a butterscotch-brown, mille fleur hen with splashes of black and white upon her soft feathers. Ironically, that very hen had been another weakling like our Phibby. This tiny hen had struggled while attempting to escape her shell during hatching. Many hours had passed after she first poked a hole through the shell, she had gotten no further and was obviously too weak to manage alone. I couldn't stand it; the idea of a chick making it that far in its development and dying at the last moment was not acceptable to me. I peeled the chick out of its shell. This required finesse. The yolk within the shell had dried all over the outside of the chick; sticking the chick to itself as well as its shell. Her little head was stuck to her wing as though glued. The shell was stuck to the chick, and the whole conglomeration was all a sticky mess. I used paper towels soaked in warm water to soften the gluey goop, removing one small piece of shell at a time, careful not to peel the chick's skin off with the egg shell. There were three chicks at the end of the hatch that all had this same problem. Two out of three survived after I employed my soaking and bathing maneuver to free them.

From this moment on, Millie and The Itsy Bitsy Tiny One are inseparable. Although she plays with three or four chicks at a time, she always has "her baby" in one hand. I set up a portable dog pen under the shade of our sweet gum tree so she can let them down to run around in a safe space. She is as gentle with them as a lovingly exuberant four year old can possibly be. There are oft-repeated reminders of "Gently! Easy with your baby, Millie. If you're too rough, I'll put it away." The word of the week is "GENTLY!" I intercede on behalf of the little hen whenever I feel the tiny darling needs a break. At these times, Millie accompanies me as I place her back inside the hutch for a bird-feed snack, a drink and a nap.

"Can I have the next smallest one, please?" She asks as we place her hen safely back with the others. Millie is content for fifteen or twenty long minutes before begging for "her baby" again.

Whenever we return to pick up The Itsy Bitsy Tiny One it shocks me to observe the hen running to us, not away from us. She likes being toted around and actually wants more of it. Millie's baby has learned to lie on its side and "stay" on command. If it tries to get back up before Millie deems it appropriate, she will "somewhat" gently push the bird down onto its side again. The chick has learned that it is just easier to stay put till released. I've seen many dogs learn that command more slowly than Millie's chick.

One might feel sorry for her chick as you hear this tale, but oddly the teensy hen loves the attention. This fact is evidenced by its behavior when Millie leaves it to play in the dog pen without her. Itsy Bitsy has other birds for company, but is not content; she wants her little girl. As Millie is standing outside the pen; her hen flies up, grabbing the wire beside Millie's shoulder, in an attempt to reach her.

Millie and her baby spent long hours in the hammock, walks around the yard or whatever Millie feels is a good idea at the time. She would sleep with that little bird if Grandma and Grandpa would allow it. We have a firm NO BIRDS IN THE HOUSE rule. We make no exceptions. Not even for The Itsy Bitsy Tiny One.

Harper also loves the birdies; however, she is not permitted to hold them. At one-and-a-half, the concept of gently holding them is beyond her comprehension. As I hold the chicks near her, she tries to squeeze their tiny necks, in a matter of milliseconds, the chick's eyes roll and it goes limp. I quickly surmise that Harper is detrimental to birdie health. She is only allowed extended-arm-length petting so she is unable to get a firm hold on them. She sure loves watching the chicks jump and play within their playpen with Millie and is content to enjoy the festivities from that safe distance.

Grandma and Grandpa are amazed at how FAST a toddler can move! Harper races from object to object with great speed and reckless abandon, confident that the adults in her life will protect her from any danger. (More accurately, unaware of any danger.) The first full day of our week-long visit together, I am "on-duty" alone while my husband is at work. I take the girls to the barn with me to feed the young birds out

there. Millie is standing by the hutch watching birds and Harper is corralled between my legs while I use both hands to remove the cover on the bird feed container. In less than a blink, Harper has squeezed out from between my legs like toothpaste from a tube. My hands are now full, so I call to her to come back (she ignores me, giggling as she runs). I drop the birdfeed and race after her. In the moment it took for all of this to happen, she manages to exit the barn, round the corner, and grasp the electric tape fencing with both hands and place the fence in her little wet mouth. Inexplicably, Harper didn't get shocked by the powerful fencer. I'm thankful for God's protection of her as that is the only explanation I can find for her not receiving a jolt. I have seen adults knocked on their back-sides by that fencer. I had bumped the fence earlier while stepping over it to feed the horses this very morning and I got zapped through my jeans. I know it's operating properly. Grandma sure learned a lesson through this. If I need both hands for anything, she has to be strapped in her stroller. I'm not as fast as a toddler!

The days of our special visit went by rapidly, very full of birdie adventures, horseback rides around the yard with Grandma on Jefé, a walk on a nearby walk trail and Millie swinging on a vine in a creek-bed, working in the garden together, playing in the sprinkler… the list goes on and on. Prior to their arrival, I found a darling book called *Ten In The Bed* by Penny Lane. The illustrations were rich with vibrant color and delightful characters. For those unfamiliar with the children's song the book is based on, each of the characters mentioned are bumped out of bed as the crowd within it "rolls over". The girls and I, sometimes with Grandpa's help, would sing the story at Harper's naptime and both their bedtimes. As soon as the book came into view, Harper began to bob her head and grin in anticipation of the fun. It was a wonderful memory maker.

All too soon our week together was over. Two exhausted grandparents returned the precious girls to their parents' care. All the D'Uccle chicks had been tamed in a way we could have never accomplished without Millie's help. The Itsy Bitsy Tiny One missed her little mistress and now flew up to sit on my shoulder in the mornings. She didn't appreciate short periods of holding; that was not what Millie had taught her to expect. If I hold her briefly, then place her down to pick up another bird, she flies up, landing atop the one I'm petting. She also flies and hops at my feet to try to "climb" up to my arms.

Each of the four D'Uccles we chose to keep is incredibly friendly. Dapper Dan; the young rooster of the group is a strong leader. He's sweet to humans while being attentive and protective of his little flock. His flock includes Phibby, Itsy Bitsy, another mille fleur hen named Sissy, and the six guinea keets they all "roomed" with in the hutch. The old adage is true; birds of a feather DO flock together. The group that starts out together usually stays together. It is important when adding new birds to a flock that you add more than one so they already have a "mini-flock" to start with. This makes them more secure and less of a target for predators or pecking from the established flock. The one exception to this rule might be the addition of a rooster to a group; roosters seem to have the confidence and bravado to find their way into a flock.

The guinea keets have been pecked and cuffed by the adult guineas, so they don't want to be part of that group. They seem to think they're chickens and they are inseparable from the chicks. They even stand in the big doorway of the chicken coop, lined up with the chicks awaiting a turn to be held. Once I pick them up, they seem alarmed and confused as though they didn't know this was what they were signing up for. They calm down after a moment of holding and oddly return time after time, every time acting surprised at the outcome.

The experience of actually holding the guineas is a side benefit I never expected, I think I'll try to raise guineas with D'Uccles every time. Another benefit to mingling the groups is the chicks have mastered the ramp almost immediately and the guineas are following them. I've been spared the dreadful fish net birdie roundup at bedtime maneuver. Hallelujah!

Eight weeks after our weeklong visit with Millie and Harper, we have the opportunity to have them visit again. By now, Dapper Dan is a full-fledged crowing rooster. The little hens follow him with willing devotion, going wherever he directs them. They are less human-centric and more interested in the normal life of chickens. They no longer show as much interest in being cuddled by me, sometimes running away from me instead of towards me as before. I wonder what the chicks' response will be to Millie when she arrives. Her expectation will not have changed; she still imagines them as tiny chicks that desire holding. We'll soon see what happens.

The girls are back. My husband and I just picked them up. As soon as we pull into the garage Millie hurries out of her car seat by herself, not waiting for us to extricate Harper from hers. She's off in a flash to search for her birdie. We work quickly to try to catch up with her (prying a child out of the belts and buckles of a child safety seat is not a small task!). Mere moments later Millie returns to the garage, her small chicken tucked snugly under her arm.

She announces, "Look what I found. Is this the Itsy Bitsy Tiny One?"

Millie seemed a little confused but undaunted by the growth of her little friend. She comments that she's still itsy bitsy compared to the other birds. That seems to satisfy Millie's desire for tiny things. (When given a choice, Millie always gravitates to the smallest item in any group.) Apparently her birdie still loves her; she couldn't have caught her if Itsy Bitsy didn't want to be held.

Itsy and Millie are once again inseparable. Itsy is less enamored with the holding than she was when she was younger, but she still partakes in tricycle rides with Millie. When she's had enough cuddle-time, Itsy squirms to signal her desire to be set free. Millie reluctantly releases her for a short respite. They reunite several times each day. I am amazed at the sweet nature of this gentle bird. What a good sport she is. (It should be noted that Itsy Bitsy is becoming harder to catch as the visit continues. She seems to believe that there is such a thing as TOO MUCH love!)

The visit with our special girls ends all too soon. My husband and I resume the usual daily activities of caring for all the birds as well as the rest of the crazy variety of critters who own us. The chicks continue to grow up day by day as youngsters are prone to do. All too soon they will be grownups, they may forget the richness of their early chick-childhood, but there are two tiny girls who will never forget the fun times they had raising chicks.

A friend recently had an extra rooster from a bantie hatch at her farm. She feared for the little fella's safety with her mature rooster who was confined with him. She asked me if he might come to free-range at my house. I of course said yes. She delivered him in a plastic dog kennel where he stayed till birdie bedtime. Once all the birds had settled in and all was quiet within the chicken house, I placed him gently in a nesting box by himself to wait till morning.

Transitioning a new bird overnight is usually pretty straightforward… usually. But when morning came and the new rooster saw the open door of the chicken coop, he was GONE. He dashed into the wood pile. After that glimpse, I couldn't locate him for two days, during which time we had rain. I was glad that at least he would have something to drink, and I placed some bird feed near the wood pile for him, in case that was where he still was. I was concerned about the temperature drop to nine degrees that was predicted for tomorrow. I didn't want him out in the harsh elements where he might freeze or where any local predators might pick him off.

Finally, on day three, he poked his wary head out from the wood pile. By the second time he peeked out I had devised a plan to capture him and confine him in the coop where I was certain he could come to no harm from wild animals and could adjust to the other birds that would now be his companions. I was waiting with my trusty fish-net and a plastic dog kennel. After several foiled attempts at netting him, he retreated again to the safety of the wood pile. No doubt scared stiff.

I set the dog kennel on the ground dejectedly and left to run errands, worrying about how to help him. After returning from my trip to town, I gazed out to see the sweet little rooster inside the dog kennel. Outside the dog kennel was our large rooster, guarding the door to the kennel, probably warning the young rooster not to look at his girls. I was astounded at my good fortune. He'd caught himself. What a relief, he's safe now.

I placed his kennel inside the chicken house filled with hay to bed down in. My thought is to keep him safe in the kennel until morning and then release him. He will be safe inside the walls of the chicken coop where no predators can reach him and safe from the attacks of the other birds while they get accustomed to his presence with them. I surmised that the big rooster or the other adult birds must have harassed and intimidated him early the first morning before I opened the door. I believe the established birds had frightened him causing him to flee in terror to the wood pile. I am so happy that everything is coming together to keep him safe as a member of our little flock.

When I arrived in the morning I found the predicted frigid weather had come. My poor tiny rooster had gotten too cold and died. I was heartbroken. I had intended to help him, but I had made a mistake. I hadn't considered all the possible ramifications of the solution I chose for helping him. It's all very obvious now, he needed the warmth of the other birds to survive, but since they hadn't been welcoming to him I had felt he should be isolated from them for his protection. I felt so guilty; I had killed him. I cried and cried.

I had really wanted him; his little life mattered to me. I had been looking forward to watching his coloring develop as he matured and hearing his first awkward attempts at crowing. I had meant it all for the best. Now none of that could ever happen.

I kept reviewing the details in my head. I said to myself, "Why didn't you leave him in the woodpile? Why didn't you let him out of the kennel before dark so he could huddle with the other birds for warmth? If you hadn't done this and you had done that, *if only, if only…*" I ruminated on my tortured thoughts all day long. Finally, later in the day, while praying, I recalled some dear families I know of who have lost children; some to accident, others to illness, still others to suicide. My loss paled in comparison. I had only lost a bird. As I thought of those families, I considered the questions that I feel sure they struggle with. All the questions: *Why did I let them go there? Why didn't I help them? I should have done this and not done that.* I cannot begin to imagine their daily agony. But on that day, as I found myself asking why, I became more aware of the pain they must experience. Now I pray for them much more often than I did before. I know God cares about their pain and I know He hears me. Perhaps my prayers for them will help them through an especially hard day. I believe that the tiny rooster's death was not wasted; for when I think of him, I pray for them.

Beyond the hard moments, I never could have imagined what fun I could experience raising these silly birds. If I had known how entertaining they would be, I would have gotten them years ago! Along with the visual pleasure obtained, I've also learned many important lessons as I've observed them. I find myself enjoying the little, simple pleasures more than I did before embarking on this fowl life.

I'm learning to slow my often frenzied pace; to pause long enough to enjoy what's unfolding around me. I'm becoming more aware that to look away means I might miss an important moment. After all, what is life but a series of moments? Each one valuable on its own merit. Some of the moments are joyous, some sad, but each one is nonetheless important. I need to embrace every single one as the treasure it is.

I also believe that a life must be observed in order to be remembered well. When I invest the time it takes to observe the lives around me, I demonstrate how much I value them. By chronicling their stories in my memory, I preserve mental snapshots of their life-story to be relived again and again. Recalling the behaviors of each individual bird, whether it be chicken or guinea, helps to keep them alive in my heart, forever remembered. The life of a bird is so fleeting; what an abundance of time I've been granted in comparison. I want to use my time wisely, savoring each tiny second as the gift it truly is. I look forward to each new day in expectation of what it might hold. Sometimes our yesterdays were full of heartache, but today is a new day.

A wise doctor I met said something that has stuck with me. He was talking with a family who felt that mistakes had been made in their daughter's previous medical care that had compromised her future health. After assuring them that he felt her care had not been faulty, the doctor said, "We cannot go backwards, but we can go forwards." What empowering words! There's no way to reverse yesterday, but we have the power and freedom to go forward. Each new day is fresh and clean just waiting for us to find the treasures within it. What a rich, full life I'm blessed to live. I can't wait to see what unfolds today.

Things I've Learned From Bird Ownership

- God watches over all the birds, not just the sparrows.
- Accept yourself; look in the mirror with appreciation.
- Savor the moment.
- Don't hold things too tightly.
- Animals are one way God shows me He loves me.
- Play and be silly.
- Run to win.
- Everyone has a role to play in the group.
- Live life with a purpose.
- Gentle leadership is best.
- Roll around in the dirt, it's a great exfoliant.
- Be careful who you follow.
- Discouragement can come any day.
- Dogs don't think like people do.
- Love with all you've got.
- Even if it hurts, love is worth the pain.
- Life is a journey, not a destination.
- Don't grieve too long; you'll miss the joy that's coming next.
- Show compassion to your friends.
- Life is short; so enjoy every moment!
- Observe and value the lives around you.

I've also learned many things from dog ownership. My next book, *Buffy, The Pit Bull Ambassador*, will share those experiences.